MONEY AND POLITICS

WITHDRAWN

STUDIES IN
POLITICAL
SCIENCE

MONEY AND POLITICS

By Jasper B. Shannon

University of Nebraska

Random House

New York

First Printing

Library of Congress Catalog Card Number: 59-6788

Manufactured in the United States of America
by The Colonial Press Inc., Clinton, Mass.

PREFACE

This study is the outgrowth of the author's membership in the Committee on Political Parties of the American Political Science Association. He was chairman of a sub-committee on party finance of the second committee on parties, 1950-1953. The committee was terminated before the work of the subcommittee had been completed.

In 1954-5, the writer held a Fulbright Research Scholar grant from the United States Educational Foundation in Norway. The University of Kentucky Research Fund and the University of Nebraska Research Council have made additional grants to make possible completion of this investigation. To each of these I now express my profound thanks.

JASPER B. SHANNON

Lincoln, Nebraska

CONTENTS

I

The Broad Nature of the Problem

Civilization grows by reducing the areas where violence is dominant. When force diminishes, fraud frequently succeeds as a determinant of policy. Neither violence nor fraud has ever been totally eliminated but their effectiveness has been confined and reduced. In law, violence, by its nature, is easier to prove than fraud and the same is true in politics. For the student of government as for the lawyer the issue is not primarily moral but scientific and legal. When is an act that of an official (sovereign agent) and when that of someone who controls the acts of the official? To point out that political fraud, like sin, is omnipresent is no answer to the problem any more than the fact that disease is present is any answer to the physician who seeks a diagnosis of cause and effect. The real inquiry is to diagnose the nature of the infection before any prescription can be made. First, the student seeks to analyze the elements involved.

In mid-twentieth century, at least two theories of the nature of an industrial society are contesting for dominance in the world. It is scarcely necessary to suggest that human survival itself may depend upon the reconciliation of the two dogmas. One of these ideologies contends that economy and the state are one—indivisible and inseparable.[1] The state according to this view is simply the agent or tool of the economic forces of production. The other view, advocated by political democrats, is that the state and the economy can live side by side in a kind of idealistic monogamy with neither partner dominating the other. This condition is called a free society. The dynamic forces which originate in a society are transmitted to the state by voluntary associations called political parties. These associations of free men present their respective values to citizens, called collectively the electorate (voters), who make repeated choices of policies (values) and officials (politicians) to operate the machinery of the state.

A condition precedent for an election is the free circulation of propaganda (ideas, values, doctrines) among which the voters may choose. One of the merits of this method of determining policies, it is contended, is the emphasis upon reason and thought. The more choices people have to make the more they have to analyze facts and conflicting values, and the higher the level of intelligence they will reach. Political democracy is at once a process of decision-making and a method of education[2]—literally drawing out the human mind to its fullest potentialities. This way of reason, intelligence, and choice stands in contrast with systems where the voter is left only the dubious alternative of rejection or acquiescence in predetermined selections of officials and values. Perhaps somewhat oversimplified, this is the issue upon which man may ultimately annihilate himself. The advocates of Marxism and the apostles of Fascism alike suppress, as a first step to totalitarian ascendancy, competing political parties. If Russia allowed "free" elections in the satellite countries, especially Poland and Hungary, the cold war would thaw. The United States has taken to Germany and Japan the doctrine of political parties and both by persuasion and stronger methods has sought to impose this conception of government upon the losers of the last war.

In moments of political ecstasy the western world glorifies democracy, liberty, freedom, and free enterprise but in times of gloomy introspection there is cynical criticism of parties and politicians, the practical means of attaining democratic values. In these hours of doubt, all politicians are considered dishonest and democracy a farce. Losers in elections, frequently, if not almost always, proclaim that they were defeated, not by majority will, but by money which either directly or indirectly destroyed the true will of the majority. In periods of democratic despondency, elections appear to observers to be a kind of auction in which sovereignty goes to the highest bidder. Inadvertently, democrats acquiesce in the dogma of the opponents of political parties that economic forces control the political ones. In an orgy of masochism, the major premise of democracy's adversaries is proclaimed to the world by its friends. Both the cynical and the unsophisticated mutter aloud that all wars are "the rich man's war and the poor man's fight." This is sometimes a fatal democratic Achilles' heel in propaganda battles. Here is a fruitful avenue by which ideologically unprepared troops, either as warriors or as prisoners, may be brain-washed into accepting enemy propaganda.

In our contemporary Peloponnesian wars, in which subversion and internal conflict are as important as in external and interstate wars, students of government, as well as citizens, need to analyze, to diagnose, and if possible to prescribe. As in medicine, no purely localized examination will suffice. The entire political physiology—its environment as well as its metabolic evolution—is essential to clarity and accuracy.

First of all, fraud is not only a disease of political democracies but may operate in other kinds of governments. Certainly Nazism was shot through with the subversion of sovereignty by cash. Communist countries are not free from it, but the concern of this study is basically with political democracies. For practical purposes, all adults are enfranchised. Fraud, or subterfuge, either legal or extralegal, in certain areas prevents the exercise of the franchise, but this is a part of the process under study. The franchise was granted largely upon the basis of a loosely interpreted conception of the equality of all mankind stemming from John Locke's broadly stated contentions and their propagandistic expression through the Declaration of Independence. The first basic assumption was that *all* men were interested in public affairs and the second that *all* men were competent to make informed judgments upon issues of public policy. These premises have never been confirmed by scientific proof; in fact, there is abundant evidence to the contrary. We enfranchised first and undertook to educate afterward. Moreover, we assumed the educability of all those who have been enfranchised.

II

The United States Experience: To 1916

The United States has been confronted from its very beginning with the problem of the interrelation of economic and political forces. How far do economic motivations determine political behavior? The very genesis of the constitution itself was involved.[1] The Supreme Court of the United States took a "realistic" attitude when it refused to look behind a legislative record to determine what motives controlled legislative action.[2] From the date of its origin until the present day the repeated "issue" of nearly every campaign has been one of "honesty and integrity" in government. Translated into the language of political science this means that the chief question is whether private economic ends (the satisfaction of private wants) or a general good (a conception of the public need) is the determinant of public policy.[3]

The fact that the United States is a new country with an abundance of natural resources has been central in most of the situations which have arisen. The objective of those seeking to purchase sovereignty has been to obtain private control of the public domain. First, it was speculation in lands and land grants and included the United States government's relations with Indians. The vast riches of America, its wealth of precious metals, timber, mineral deposits, and especially oil, have been the source of disruption of its ethical traditions. The more these scarce resources tended to create profitable monopolies, thereby giving to private bodies the power to tax (usually regarded as a perquisite of sovereignty), the greater has been the temptation to use economic power directly or indirectly to control national policy.[4]

Credit institutions have been another avenue of close connection between economic and political power. The struggle over rechartering the United States bank, coming as it did at a time when the franchise was being extended to include larger bodies of voters, was the center of political strategy. The bank used its credit to develop avenues of propaganda to influence the voters, and the party in power employed public office (patronage) and public business (printing) as a weapon of retaliation. In this fashion the public service (bureaucracy) tended for many years to become a tool of party rather than of the state.[5]

The direct connection between political campaigning and public policy did not emerge very clearly in the first quarter century of American political history. However, as an opposition party was being formed, its leader, Thomas Jefferson, took steps to establish newspapers as organs of party propaganda. He collected funds from his friends in Philadelphia in 1799, though the amount was "disappointing." [6] The following year he himself advanced an additional fifty dollars to help publish party pamphlets.[7]

This early government by the leadership of a landed elite was expensive to its members. Jefferson was nearly insolvent at the end of his presidency.[8]

However, James Monroe was to share a similar fate for he "literally bankrupted himself in the public service." [9] Congress voted him thirty thousand dollars after he left office but the amount was insufficient for his needs.

The expansion of the electorate enhanced the power of the party press. The first legend of the military hero turned party chieftain in the image of the common man was in no small part the creation of party journalists.[10]

Between 1824 and 1828 the franchise was extended and all but two of the states voted directly for presidential candidates instead of allowing the legislature to make the choice.[11] These potential sovereigns had to be reached by propaganda and organization. Either job hunters or money had to be found to "engineer" the consent of the governed. Likewise, the resort to personalities was bitter and disgraceful. To the Jackson cry of "corrupt bargain" between Adams and Clay, the defenders of the administration replied by calling Jackson an "adulterer" and a "murderer." To the office of the President of the United States early in 1828 came a solicitor for funds to aid in the fiercely contested gubernatorial election in Kentucky. John Quincy Adams with remarkable insight and some foresight told his inner self what he saw:

> Bailey of Massachusetts came and passed a couple of hours with me this evening. His object was to make a proposition in the first instance not very distinctly disclosed, but which I chose immediately to understand and to meet in a manner altogether explicit. He ultimately informed me that it had been suggested to him by Mr. Webster.
>
> I answered that there was a sentiment expressed first by the late Mr. Lowndes, much repeated since by General Jackson and his friends, though not practised upon by them, but hitherto invariably observed by me that the Presidency of the United States was an office neither to be sought or declined. To pay money for securing it directly or indirectly, was in my opinion incorrect in principle. This was my first and decisive reason for declining such a contribution. A second reason was that I could not even command a sum of five thousand dollars without involving myself in debt for it; and a third was, that if I once departed from my principle and gave money there was no rule, either of expediency or of morality, which would enable me to limit the amount of expenditure which I ought to incur. I could certainly appro-

priate half a million of dollars to the same object without transcending any law, and with as much propriety as I could devote five thousand to the election of a Governor of Kentucky.

I note as a remarkable incident this proposition to me to contribute five or ten thousand dollars to carry the election of a Governor and Legislature of Kentucky. The mode of expenditure is by the circulation of newspapers, pamphlets, and handbills. It is practiced by all parties, and its tendency is to render elections altogether venal. The coincidence of Mr. Clark's proposal that I should write a pamphlet in answer to Ingham's slanders about my accounts with Mr. Clay's opinion that Mr. Webster, if he insisted, would be appointed to the mission to Great Britain, and with Mr. Webster's proposal that I should sport five or ten thousand dollars upon the election of a Governor in Kentucky, is perhaps all accidental; but in the operations of parties objects of great dissimilarity to each other are often connected by imperceptible links together.[12]

Secretary of State Henry Clay and Daniel Webster were more practical men. Clay urged Adams to use the patronage while he received funds from Webster, apparently collected in Massachusetts, and sent the money to Hammond, one of the most "virulent" purveyors of the adultery charges against Jackson.[9] Hammond's paper was the best published for "our cause," wrote Clay, but Hammond "is poor, disinterested, and proud." He was worthy of encouragement and patronage. "The only assistance he would receive would be in the extension of his subscription list. Perhaps he might receive a present of a new set of types." Hammond did not know of Clay's interest, but the Kentuckian inquired meaningfully "cannot there be something done for him in your quarter?"[13]

Shortly afterward, the Secretary of State wrote Webster that the matter of Hammond had better wait, for a "better mode of accomplishing the object in view has presented itself."[13] However the subject was pursued in another letter shortly afterward:

The course adopted by the Opposition, in the dissemination of newspapers and publications against the administration, and supporting presses leaves to its friends no other alternative than that of following their example, so far at least as to circulate information among the people.

He commented upon the bright prospects in Virginia, but saw the danger of losing "Mr. Pleasants and the *Whig* from the want of pecuniary means. What ought to be done?"

Answering his own question, Clay suggested:

It seems to me that our friends who have ability should contribute a fund for the purpose of aiding the Cause; and if that be deemed advisable, the appeal should be made in the large cities where alone the Capital is to be found. You stated, I think, last winter that such a fund would be raised, and that I was authorized to address you on the subject. I have not felt that I ought to avail myself of the authority, fearing that your means might be encroached on too much. As for myself, if it were otherwise proper [He was the Secretary of State], I am too poor. I have not the pecuniary ability.

The way to help was to buy additional copies of papers.

The best form of affording aid to struggling presses is to supply it, and require that a number of additional papers shall be circulated gratis, bearing some proportion to the circulation made.[14]

Webster apparently acted, for a few days later Clay told him that his letters were safe since only Clay and one clerk, who was dependable, opened his letters.

I am glad that you are enabled to procure a contribution for the *Whig* to the amount mentioned in your last letter. It will afford at least present relief, and until some other arrangement can be made.

Clay, probably worried over his role in collecting money, suggested that the funds be sent to another.

I would prefer (if you have no objection) that the sum should be remitted to the Honorable J. S. Johnston,[15] who is here, animated by the greatest zeal in the cause, doing more than any other person that I know, and who is in habit of correspondence with the Editors of the *Whig*. He knows the situation of the Editors, and has contributed himself handsomely to their relief. He will immediately pass the sum to its destination.[13]

A year later, just before Adams's defeat, Clay again mentioned the topic of money. Speaking of his home state, Kentucky, Clay declared:

I have heard of the safe reception there of what you sent. All has been done, and will continue to be done, that honorable men can or ought to do.[13]

A month later Clay in an election *post mortem* made reference to personalities.

We are of the majority, in regard to measures; we are in the minority in respect to the person designated as C.——magistrate.[13]

This correspondence at the very genesis of a new realignment of politics upon a two party basis sets out clearly the problems of financing the point of view of a party. The voters were to be propagandized with the printing press as one of the chief means of reaching the electorate.

Four years later, the United States Bank whose recharter was advocated by Clay, Jackson's opponent, subsidized propaganda against Jackson. Curiously enough, the Bank officials, believing the Bank a popular institution, circulated thousands of copies of Jackson's veto message thereby inadvertently financing the enemy. This is an early example of collateral propaganda by a business corporation.[16] Within a period of two years (1830-1832) the Bank spent $42,000 in publication of literature favorable to the Bank.[17] According to one view this was the beginning of "one of the greatest struggles between democracy and the money power." [18]

A few years later, in 1839, Whig merchants contributed $8,000 "in a bandana handkerchief" on request of Thurlow Weed.[19]

Another glimpse of the problem of party finance occurred in 1844, when Clay was last the Whig nominee for president. A friendly writer from Hamilton county, Ohio, declared:

> ORGANIZATION is the great instrument of efficient and successful effort. Organization of counties, townships, wards, precincts and even *neighborhoods*—families: organization *at once* Without Delay—with organization such as this everything may be done, without it nothing.[20]

Perhaps the Whigs' successful mobilization of opinion in 1840 furnished the motive for the enthusiastic proposal to organize the Whig party on a pattern resembling religious groups. At any rate, the suggestion demonstrates the role of organization and money both in religion and politics.

> I have got two or three great ideas for our National organization and enrollment which I have not time to unfold fully in this letter. . . . In the course of this winter, I want to set in motion a system of organization throughout New York, New England,—and afterwards, in the same model, through Pennsylvania, Ohio, etc. This is to form a Whig local association with *weekly* meetings in each village and each school district of the state, with weekly addresses, weekly pecuniary contributions, and weekly distributions of pamphlets, documents, papers, etc.
>
> The fundamental idea is borrowed from the religious organizations of the day. The model of my primary local association is the Christian Church. The officers, the exercises, the exhortations, the singing, the weekly meetings (on Wednesday night), the enrolment of members, the contributions, and all are to be on the primitive apostolic model, nearly as presented in the Congregational churches of New England. Then I want itinerant lectures, political preachers going about in regular circuits, next spring and summer, on the Methodist plan,—changing from village to village and from county to county and from state to state, alternating

with each other so as to keep each place regularly supplied with a new speaker, and thus making a small original stock of ideas go a great ways. The officers of each local association to be a President, Secretary, Registrar, Treasurer, and marshall,—a choir of regular singers to be also kept up. These little unit associations are to be mutually fraternized and affiliated to County, District—and state central associations, with regular and definite means of communication, for the concentration and diffusion of political meetings or mass meetings to rear at stated times as a part of the system, monthly, quarterly, etc. As may seem best, each association then appearing in emulous display of strength and zeal, marshalled and led each by its own marshall. Each of all the hundreds of thousands of members of these associations will also make a weekly contribution of *one cent* to the great cause of our "church militant." ONE CENT weekly, *no more* and no less, rich and poor all to be on one level, with no individual display of difference in means,—and each one receiving a noble equivalent in the distribution of papers. We had last fall 186,000 Whig votes in the state of New York. We have really 220,000 Whig voters. But 200,000 cents weekly will go far towards paying expenses.

I am also going to get up a Clay button, to be brought into fashion first at Baltimore, Maryland and to be worn on every Whig coat in the United States. We shall then have by the 4 of July 1,500,000 men in the Clay uniform.[21]

Needless to say, this wild dream was not attained in 1844, or subsequently for that matter. It does illustrate the ideal of a political party supported by its membership on a wide base.

However, in 1848, Weed furnished funds for the Taylor nomination campaign in Ohio and other states.[19] The Whigs were reported to have "oceans of money" in Pennsylvania and "committees of visitation" made house to house canvasses.[22]

The fiscal basis of the Whig party is more accurately demonstrated by an intimate letter of a former Whig cabinet colleague and United States senator from Delaware,

to the Attorney General in the Fillmore Cabinet. He was
seeking a minor naval appointment for a junior member of
the DuPont family. In confidence, he declared:

> Now, my dear Crittenden, these Duponts have spent a for-
> tune for the Whig party, and have never received a favor
> from it, for they never desired any,—they have been the chief
> prop and support of our party ever since its origin; they did
> more to build it up, originally, than any other family in the
> State, and but for their powerful influence we should have
> sent two Locofoco senators to Congress for the last twenty
> years.[23]

The Democrats in the 1850's likewise were beginning
to depend upon men of wealth to advance their cause. In
1850, August Belmont, wealthy representative of the house
of Rothschild collected funds to establish a newspaper to
support the presidential ambitions of James Buchanan.
Belmont himself contributed $10,000.[24] In 1852, the newly
organized Democratic National Committee attempted to
raise money to promote the cause of their candidate. They
were not too successful even though Samuel J. Tilden lent
his aid, but ultimately, "at the opportune moment Belmont
stepped in and contributed a large sum to the National
Committee. Thus the matter of funds was taken care of." [24]
In fact, August Belmont became chairman of the Democratic National Committee, a position he held for twelve
years. His house was the center of the Committee where
its meetings were held from 1860 through 1868.[25]

According to one account, in a predominantly rural constituency a Whig candidate running for Congress in 1846
found his race inexpensive. The friends of the Whig
nominee in prairie Illinois, contributed $200 to enable him
to campaign. Successful, the candidate gave back to the
donors $199.25. In this version Abraham Lincoln returned
this sum to his friend, an agent of the party supporters.

> "I did not need the money," he said. "I made the canvass on
> my own horse; my entertainment, being at the houses of
> friends, cost me nothing; and my only outlay was 75 cents

for a barrel of cider, which some farm hands insisted I should treat them to." [26]

Another study casts doubt upon this.[27]

However, the race for the Senate in 1858 was another story. In fact, Lincoln had accepted a contribution of two or three hundred dollars towards his expenses in campaigning in 1856, and, in 1858, he applied to the same donor for help. Lincoln wrote that he had had authority to draw in 1856 for a sum not exceeding $500: "I see clearly that such a privilege would be more available now than it was then. The outcome we do not know." [28]

At the end of the campaign, Lincoln wrote that he was "absolutely without money now for even household purposes." Since he had been the nominee, however, he thought he should not be "over nice" so he pledged a contribution to pay the expenses of the Republican Committee. His contribution amounted to more than $500 not counting his personal expenses for travel, hotel, and sundries.[29] He had to go back to his law practice to compensate himself.[30]

In 1860, Lincoln, a dark horse candidate from Illinois, was willing to pay $100 as part of the expenses of a potential delegate, a political and personal friend, to the Chicago convention. Lincoln wrote:

> I cannot enter the ring on the money basis—first, because in the main it is wrong; and secondly, I have not and cannot get the money. I say in the main the use of money is wrong; but for certain objects in a political contest the use of some is both right and indispensable. With me as with yourself, this long struggle has been one of great pecuniary loss. I now distinctly say this: "If you shall be appointed a delegate to Chicago, I will furnish one hundred dollars to bear the expense of the trip." [31]

Although his friend did not become a delegate, Lincoln agreed to pay the $100 on his expenses anyway. Apparently, Lincoln paid this partisan supporter something, but the manuscript is mutilated so it is not clear how much.[32] When he became President, Lincoln appointed him to a comfortable federal job and subsequently made him a United States Federal District Judge. His conduct was such that he was removed shortly before impeachment proceedings were instituted.[31]

Lincoln likewise secretly bought a small weekly German newspaper in Illinois. He turned it over to an editor who agreed to follow Republican policy and publish his paper both in German and English. The paper cost Lincoln $400.[33] After his election, large numbers of editors who had supported him were appointed to office.

The Railsplitter's nomination was clinched by the promise of a cabinet job to Simeon Cameron, the beginning of Pennsylvania's strategic bargaining position in Republican conventions maintained by Quay, Penrose, and their successors until the present.[34]

Some of Lincoln's friends paid for the expenses of the committee which obtained his nomination. A good portion of the costs was for wine and whiskey and brandy.[27] Financing Lincoln's first campaign for the presidency was four times as costly as James Buchanan's successful effort in 1856. The costs rose from less than $25,000 to more than $100,000.[35] After his nomination, ten of Lincoln's friends pledged five hundred dollars each to take care of campaign expenses. When this sum was exhausted the donors added more until their total outlay was $12,000.[27] A close banker-lawyer friend of Seward's added $3,000 to Lincoln's campaign fund.[36]

Judge David Davis, the political realist, who did so much to effect Lincoln's nomination, deeply concerned about doubtful Indiana, wrote the master strategist, Thurlow Weed, asking for more money, concluding: *"Men work better with money in hand. . . . I believe in God's Providence in this Election, but at the same time we should keep our powder dry."* [37]

In strategic Pennsylvania, Carl Schurz wooed German support for a fee of $600. Money came from New England. The Democrats charged hundreds and thousands of dollars

were being spent. One Republican source admitted $100,-
000 was sent into the Keystone state by the New York
Republican Committee.

The Democrats were divided. Breckinridge was supported
by office holders under Buchanan while Douglas found it
almost impossible to raise funds since the New York
merchants felt he had no chance to win.[36] August Belmont
wrote the Illinois Senator:

> My efforts to collect money in the City have met with but
> little success, and unless we can give to our merchants and
> politicians some *assurance of success* I fear that it will be
> impossible to raise the necessary funds for our campaign.
> There is at present an apathy and indifference, of which it
> is difficult to form an idea—the opinion has gained ground,
> that nothing can prevent the election of Lincoln and that it
> is consequently useless to spend any money in a hopeless
> cause—others, who usually contribute freely to our funds, are
> afraid to lose their southern customers by siding with us. I
> have made a most *urgent personal appeal* to G. Low, but
> he positively declines: the fact is he wants another Republican
> Legislature in Albany, which will help him in his schemes
> to plunder the public. Aspinwall and others, upon whom I
> calculated, keep also aloof. . . .
>
> *My opinion is that if we could only demonstrate to all
> those lukewarm and selfish money-bags, that we have a strong
> probability to carry the State of New York, we might get
> from them the necessary sinews of war.* This, I think, can be
> done and no time ought to be lost in going to work to bring
> it about.[36]

These actions demonstrate eloquently the change in
political ethics in the thirty years between John Quincy
Adams and Abraham Lincoln. The price of mass participation was organization. This in turn produced the professional who had to be paid either in money or patronage or
both.

During the Civil War itself, Jay Cooke, the outstanding
financier of the Federal government's war effort, gave
"pecuniary aid" to the ambitions of Chief Justice Salmon P.
Chase, who had been Secretary of the Treasury, to replace

Lincoln as the Republican nominee. These efforts included planting a magazine article, publishing a Chase biography, and purchasing a newspaper to advance the cause.[38]

After Lincoln was renominated in 1864, Cooke subscribed $1,000 to Lincoln's campaign.

After the Civil War the relationship of men of great wealth and office holders became even closer. Jay Cooke, liberally but grumblingly, twice supported General Grant, the military hero, for the presidency. In 1868, Cooke gave about ten per cent of the total ($20,000 of the $200,000 raised by the Republicans).[39] Cooke was careful before he contributed his money. Writing to his brother of the requests from various committees, he asserted:

> I shall for the present do nothing and give not a penny to any, and request you to take the same position. If the Republican party is to turn repudiators I will desert them. The whole matter must be at once understood before I give any money. The scoundrels deserve hanging for the irreparable injury they are doing to this glorious nation.[38]

A student of the campaign of 1868, writing of the Republican advantage states: "They were successful in exacting large sums from land-grant railroad promoters, and from leaders in finance and industry who, enriched by the war, were hopeful of future favors."

Besides Cooke, large amounts were given to the Grant campaign by Vanderbilt, the Astors, A. T. Stewart and Henry Hilton.[40]

A prominent historian of the period, Oberholtzer, describes the demands of the party managers as "insolent" and declares that "never before was a candidate placed under such great obligation to men of wealth as was Grant, who was kept in the dark in this particular." [41]

Jay Cooke kept up a warm friendship with the Treasury including a one-time assistant secretary of the treasury who became a long-time secretary of the Republican National Committee, William E. Chandler.[42]

August Belmont, as Chairman of the Democratic National Committee, was one of eight leading donors to the Democratic fund. These prominent Democrats signed a contract with August Schell, Chairman of the Democratic National Executive Committee, to pay $10,000 each. Besides Belmont and Schell, Samuel J. Tilden, Charles O'Conor and Cyrus H. McCormick joined in the agreement "to defray the just and lawful expenses of circulating documents and newspapers, perfecting organizations, etc., to promote the election of Seymour and Blair." [43]

Perhaps it was significant of the difference in point of view of the two parties that the largest contribution to the Democrats, $40,000, came from an advertiser of patent medicine.[39]

The New York *Tribune* commented that the donor knew "who his friends are, and where his patrons came from." He was willing to back the Democrats with a wager of a million dollars.[40] Federal office holders were assessed but with Johnson, a Democrat, in the White House it was uncertain which party would be the beneficiary. The acting treasurer of the Democrats undertook to raise sums for the Democrats while the two top officials of the Republican National Committee and the chairman of the two Republican congressional committees asked for voluntary offerings. The attitude towards the usefulness of money is shown by the suggestion that a sum be set up to bribe the Washington correspondents *en masse*.[40]

In 1872, Jay Cooke donated at least $50,000 and perhaps more to the Republicans. Though he complained, Cooke promised:

> You know very well that we shall do everything we can for Mr. Delano and Gen. Grant and all our folks in Washington. If necessary for you to have more money, of course, you shall have it.[39]

Contractors with the Interior Department and Indian traders gave their share, while the Secretary of War supplied the names of additional contractors for solicitation.

Of course, office holders were assessed, but Cooke's gifts represented about 25 per cent of the total.[39]

In 1876, a frequent contributor to Democratic campaign funds, Samuel J. Tilden, himself, was the presidential nominee, but he spent only about $100,000 of his own money.[44]

The Republicans continued in power with their usual $200,000 expenditure. The Democrats probably spent less, about $150,000 in all.[45]

However, in the final result, money played a significant part but how decisive is not certain.

In 1880, Garfield, his reputation already slightly tarnished by *Crédit Mobilier* and other financial dealings, begged for employer pressure on workers and feverishly inquired about assessment of governmental employees.[46] Covertly, he sought the support of "Mr. Rockafeller" (sic). It was not "means" he wanted but the oil magnate's influence in the crucial state of Indiana.[47] A man of modest means, Garfield had to seek the fiscal aid of Cleveland friends to meet his entertainment obligations. One friend gave $1,000 to Garfield personally with no strings tied.[46]

During the late 1880's and early 1890's the burden of party expenditures, partly as a result of Civil Service reform, gradually shifted from public employees to corporation interests with Standard Oil, the Pennsylvania Railroad and steel companies giving regularly.[48] "Frying the Fat" was introduced.

The American system of protection advocated by the Republican party was to furnish a supply of funds. The president of a high tariff group proposed to put the manufacturers of Pennsylvania under the fire and fry all the fat out of them.[48]

Grover Cleveland made the tariff the chief issue in 1888. The Republican National Chairman, Quay, turned a bit reluctantly to a pious merchant, John Wanamaker, a sentimental Republican, to collect campaign funds. Wanamaker agreed,

provided the National Committee would agree to the creation
of an advisory board made up of business men, with its own
treasurer, and given unrestricted power in raising and decid-
ing upon the expenditure of funds. The board should be
large and representative, covering the whole country, but its
efficiency would depend upon having a small executive committee with full power to act.[49]

Ten men in Philadelphia led by Wanamaker himself
pledged $10,000 each. "With this sum as a nucleus, and the
tariff issue as the argument, manufacturers were ap-
proached, and additional contributions were collected." [49]
Wanamaker denied that the total reached $400,000 but
acknowledged it was greater than $200,000. Wanamaker's
friendly biographer admits that "it was the largest sum
used in a presidential campaign up to that time, and the fact
that every other Republican except the head of the ticket
was defeated in New York looked suspicious." Wanamaker denied any wrong use of funds, justifying the large
expenditures on the ground of the size of the country and
a new generation of voters unfamiliar with American traditions. However, the political realist, Matthew Quay, did
not accept the version of the victor, the pious Harrison,
who attributed his triumph to Providence. The Pennsylvania politicians exclaimed: "He ought to know that Providence hadn't a damn thing to do with it." [49] At any rate,
Wanamaker became Postmaster General in Harrison's cabinet.

Writing of the campaign of 1888, a leading student of
the period after describing the tariff as the leading issue
states:

The protected industries defended themselves with their
natural weapons. They subscribed more liberally than ever
before to the Republican electoral expenses. In 1888, more
money was raised than in any previous national campaign,
and it was raised more largely from business men. Its
ability to obtain increased supplies from such sources was a
Godsend to the machine, because the spread of the movement
toward Civil Service Reform had diminished its collection

from office-holders, while at the same time the constant increase of political professionalism was making electoral campaigns more than ever expensive. Large expenditures for political purposes thereafter became the rule; and the needs of professional politicians, like other parasites, soon increased up to the level of their means of subsistence.[50]

The McKinley tariff of 1890 was frequently regarded as the pay off. The *Nation* declared that the McKinley Act was "a series of minute interferences with trade and industry for the benefit of individuals, firms and corporations" which this magazine attributed to

the wicked and unprincipled measure which that party (Republican) devised to pay the campaign debts of Quay and Wanamaker. The cash that was subscribed to elect Harrison was charged up to the American people in a gross, uncounted sum. It was to be collected by duties on tin plate, worsted cloth, carpet wool, pearl buttons, and a thousand other things that enter into the food and raiment of the people.[51]

The Democratic party also had its supporters among men of wealth. William C. Whitney, an active sponsor of Grover Cleveland in 1884, took the lead when the Democrats seemed doomed to defeat because of lack of funds. "Whitney's method was first to contribute himself and then induce others to come along who might otherwise have objected to give on their own." [52] He, himself, was third or fourth among the Democratic contributors. Cleveland, himself, lacking the ethical restraints of John Quincy Adams, contributed $10,000. All told the Democratic National Committee received $453,000.[53] Whitney became Cleveland's Secretary of the Navy and a patronage dispenser. In 1892, Whitney "encouraged" Boss Croker by putting his name in the betting pool behind Cleveland to change the betting in Cleveland's favor. Though Croker put up no money, he was paid $100,000 after the election as his share of the dividend.[52] Whitney managed Cleveland's campaign finances so well that for the first time after the

Civil War the Democrats equalled or *exceeded* the Republican money. He is asserted to have contributed as much as $250,000 himself. Whitney tried to raise $1,000,000 from businessmen alone.[52]

When W. J. Bryan captured the Democratic nomination in 1896, Whitney lent his name to the finance committee of the Gold Democrats. Other prominent Democratic contributors of the post Civil War period combined their funds against the economic heresies of Bryan.[54] In this case, party loyalty did not extend itself beyond economic interest. It remained for another successful businessman turned politician, Mark Hanna, to perfect the process of bringing business corporations to the aid of political action. In 1896, Mr. Hanna applied himself assiduously to the process of creating a President of the United States in the same manner he would have employed to manufacture a new machine in a factory. First of all, he set out to procure the nomination for William McKinley but first had to restore Mr. McKinley's personal finances.[55] In 1893, McKinley became bankrupt and his friends, especially Hanna, collected funds to pay off his debts.[56]

In the next place, he undertook systematically to nominate McKinley for President. Recognizing the changes which had ensued in the twenty years since the "understanding" which assured the election of Hayes, he used whatever means were necessary to obtain southern delegates operating from his southern home at Thomasville, Georgia.[57] McKinley's competitor, Thomas B. Reed, felt that more than hospitality and "personal attention" had been offered. Reed himself refused to be "practical" and deal with a man of great wealth, or with those who wished to bargain for offices.[58] He recognized the role of the Negro vote as a factor in Republican as well as Democratic politics.[59] In the meantime legal subterfuge and bribery had succeeded to the violence of the Ku Klux Klan as a means of keeping the Negro vote under control. Northern businessmen and their money played a part.[60] Purchasing votes and controlling the counting of ballots became a way of maintaining white civilization. Even the border states resorted to similar devices.[61] The ethics and cost of buying votes was used as a reason for disfranchisement. "Repugnance for corrupt elections was put forward everywhere as the primary reason for disfranchisement." A delegate to the Alabama Constitutional Convention of 1901, blurted out: "Now we are not begging for 'ballot reform' or anything of the sort, but we want to be relieved of purchasing the Negroes to carry elections. I want cheaper votes." [62]

The secret ballot paid for by the state instead of by the parties was gradually adopted as a device to avoid wholesale bribery and repeating. Also, permanent registration of voters and other numerous means were devised to enforce "honesty" in elections.[63]

To William E. Chandler, who had managed partisan campaign funds in the past, the control of nominations by money was an outrage. Hanna was seeking $250,000 to nominate McKinley "which could not be used except for illegitimate purposes." He continued:

> Whatever may be said of reasonable contributions after the nomination is made, a system of using money to control Republican nominations would be scandalous in the highest degree and fatal to all attempts to maintain purity and honesty of party organization.[39]

Hanna's chief biographer contends that none of the $100,000 which Hanna personally contributed was used illegitimately.[50] McKinley virtually refused to barter cabinet positions for support.[50] In the campaign that followed, Hanna inaugurated a mass appeal propaganda which became a prototype for future campaigns.[64] How much money Hanna collected and spent is not precisely known, but the sum was said to be as much as $16,000,000 by critics. Croly estimates the sum as somewhat over $3,500,000. At any rate, Hanna perfected the process by going to the sources of large money.

> The customary method of voluntary contribution, helped out by a little dunning of the protected manufacturers, was

wholly insufficient. Money in sufficient volume could not be raised locally. *The dominant issue endangered the national financial system, and the money must be collected in New York, the headquarters of national finance.*[65]

The great railroad magnate, James J. Hill, went about with Hanna, who was relatively unknown in financial quarters, and introduced him so that financial leaders would trust him. They were suspicious of ordinary politicians.

> Once they knew him, he gained their confidence. They could contribute money to his war chest, with none of the qualms which they suffered when "giving up to a regular political boss." They knew that the money would be honestly and efficiently expended in order to secure the victory of Republican candidates. Never again during the campaign of 1896 or during any campaign managed by Mr. Hanna was the National Committee pinched for cash.[50]

Bryan had no such sources of income. An appeal for funds was made by the chairman of the Democratic National Committee. "A considerable sum was realized, most of it being subscribed in small amounts." Newspapers helped. The *New York Journal,* a Hearst publication, raised the largest sum, $40,901.20, $15,000 of which came from the *Journal* itself.[66]

Hanna's expenditures shocked even Republicans.[39] This was to bear fruit later.

In 1900, Hanna repeated his successful methods. "The whole corporation interest rallied more enthusiastically than ever to the Republicans and opened its purse more liberally than ever." No distinction was drawn between big business and business in general.

> It was much more convenient to get the money needed for an effective campaign from them than from a larger number of smaller subscribers; and such was particularly the case because the smaller business men were much less conscious of their political interests and responsibilities than were their more opulent associates.[50]

Hence, Hanna turned more to Wall Street. However, he systematized contributions so that donations would be an "explicit recognition" that they "were paying for a definite service." Each corporation was expected to donate "according to its stake in the general prosperity of the country and according to its special interest in a region in which a large amount of expensive canvassing had to be done." Thus the Standard Oil Corporation had returned to it $50,000 of its $250,000 contribution as more than its 'share.'

Croly describes the system as one of "unofficial taxation" which "a certain class of business was obliged to pay, because in one way or another its prosperity and even its safety had become dependent upon the political management of the country." This system itself "remained the natural outcome of a relation between business and politics, which the politico-economic history had conspired to produce and for which in a very real sense the mass of the American people were just as much responsible as were its beneficiaries and perpetrators." Hanna removed the taint of corruption. He even returned one $10,000 contribution to a firm of Wall Street bankers because a definite service was demanded by implication. These gifts were not investments in particular favors or corruption, says Croly. They were investments in public policy.

> The men whose hands went deepest into their pockets understood in general that, if the Republicans won, the politics of the country would be managed in the interest of business— a consequence which was acknowledged by all the Republican speakers and by none so frankly as by Mark Hanna.

However, Mr. Croly continues:

> But the more the practice of assessing corporate interests for the benefit of one party was reduced to a system, the more impossible it became. The very means which were taken by business to protect itself against hostile political agitation was bound in the long run to inflame the irritation; and the more the irritation became inflamed, the greater the injury which

business would suffer when it eventually lost control. The
intimate association of business prosperity with illegal and
unfair business practices was bound to make general business,
whether innocent or guilty, pay the final costs.

Hanna's friendly biographer concludes with an expression of bewilderment:

> It is extraordinary that the hard headed men who throughout
> so many years spent so much money for political protection,
> did not realize that business could not permanently succeed
> in having its own way in politics by the use of merely busi-
> ness means and methods—without corrupting the country.[50]

The use of money not only for campaign purposes but to
purchase seats in the United States Senate developed somewhat blatantly. Two wealthy business rivals in Montana
spent huge sums, one to be elected, the other to prevent
his enemy from election. The bribery was so brazen that
a senatorial investigation compelled the purchaser to resign,
but subsequently he was chosen, and the Senator who
pressed the investigation met defeat at the hands of railroad
interests.[39]

In Colorado, the purchase of a senate seat succeeded on
the first trial.[67]

The growth of the close relationship between the economy and government was a primary cause of the rise of
the Progressive movement. Campaign contributions, the use
of money to distort legislative actions, and to pervert electoral results had become a major issue.

As early as 1873, the question of corporate wealth as a
means of controlling public policy had been raised. Robert
M. LaFollette asserted that the speech of Chief Justice
Ryan to a University of Wisconsin graduating class was
the genesis of his thinking on the entire question of money
in politics. Ryan declared:

> "There is looming up a new and dark power. . . . The accu-
> mulation of individual wealth seems to be greater than it
> ever has been since the downfall of the Roman Empire. The
> enterprises of the country are aggregating vast corporate

combinations of unexampled capital, boldly marching, not for economic conquests only, but for political power. For the first time really in our politics money is taking the field as an organized power."

[Justice Ryan then made reference to the two great railways in Wisconsin and continued]:

"The question will arise, and arise in your day, though perhaps not fully in mine, 'which shall rule—wealth or man, which shall lead—money or intellect; who shall fill public stations—educated and patriotic free men, or the feudal serfs of corporate capital.' " [68]

LaFollette's personal experiences with the power of money in politics in political conventions and in attempts to control the courts had much to do with his ultimate point of view. One solution he proposed was the direct primary as part of a "back to the people" movement.[69] In 1897, a Progressive newspaper advocated abolition of railroad passes and bribery and supported a direct primary.

In the meantime, the campaign of 1904 had again focused attention upon campaign funds. Theodore Roosevelt, according to one account, frightened with the prospect of defeat, turned to a direct and active solicitation of money for what he thought to be a failing campaign. Rejecting a suggestion of Lincoln Steffens that he depend upon small gifts of from one dollar to five dollars from small contributors, Roosevelt instead called upon two of the country's ten richest men, E. H. Harriman and Harry C. Frick, to visit him in the White House. According to one version, Frick reported: "He got down on his knees to us. We bought the son of a bitch and then he did not stay bought." [70] In his letter to Harriman, in 1904, Roosevelt certainly engaged in some remarkable language:

Now, my dear sir, you and I are practical men. . . . If you think there is any danger of your visit causing me trouble, or if you think there is nothing special I should be informed about, or no matter in which I could give aid, of course, give up the visit for the time being, and then a few weeks hence, before I write my message (to Congress) I shall get you to come down to discuss certain governmental matters not connected with the campaign.

> With great regard,
> Sincerely yours,
> Theodore Roosevelt[71]

This has the ear marks of offering a bargain to sell presidential policy in a state of the union message in exchange for campaign contributions. Harriman raised $250,000, $50,000 of which was his own contribution. Roosevelt's total campaign fund apparently was only one half as much as Hanna had collected for McKinley. Twelve days after writing his private letter to Harriman, President Roosevelt rejected a contribution from the Standard Oil Company. In a public letter, he wrote:

> I have just been informed that the Standard Oil people have contributed $100,000 to our campaign fund. This may be entirely untrue. But if true I must ask you to direct that the money be returned to them forthwith.[71]

When Roosevelt's opponent accused him of having extorted "money and blackmailed the monopolies, the President called Parker's charges 'monstrous' and 'atrociously false.' " [72]

This episode in the life of Roosevelt furnished one of the principal reasons for LaFollette's failure to support him in 1912.[73] In 1905-6, Charles E. Hughes investigated the economic practices of New York life insurance companies. He brought out reluctant testimony from a partner of J. P. Morgan and Company that New York Life gave $48,000 to Roosevelt's 1904 campaign fund and that similar donations were given by it and other companies in 1896 and 1900 to McKinley's campaign.[74] Hughes inquired if contributions to campaign funds "put the candidate more or less under a moral obligation not to attack the interest supporting him?"

> Senator Platt, leader of the New York state Republican organization, replied: That is naturally what is involved.

Hughes: But isn't that really what is involved?

Platt: I should think so.

Hughes: That is what you meant when you said that they would expect you, through your relations to the State Committee, to defend them?

Platt: Yes, sir.[74]

New York then passed legislation, drafted by Hughes, prohibiting insurance companies and other corporations from making contributions to political campaigns.[74]

In 1905, Roosevelt in a long letter to Lincoln Steffens defended his campaign tactics of 1904. He stated no one had asked any favors. He pointed out his message to Congress recommending publicity of contributions and expenditures by both national parties. He declared that it was impossible to determine the motives of the contributors:

Whether corporations should be permitted to contribute or not is doubtful. They always have been allowed to contribute, sometimes to one fund and sometimes to another.

He reviewed the costs of recent campaigns:

My campaign cost a great deal of money. It did not cost as much as either of McKinley's, or as Cleveland's '92 campaign. I doubt if it cost more than Parker's, but it probably cost more than Bryan's or than Harrison's '92 campaign.

After his long rationalization of his behavior and that of his managers, Roosevelt added in longhand as a final justification:

P. S. Remember that the wrong lies not in receiving the contribution, large or small, but in exercising directly or indirectly, by improper pressure to get it, or in making an [sic] promise, express or implied, as to any consideration being given for it; by the action or inaction of any government official.[71]

He did not take kindly to the suggestion of returning funds from tainted sources, particularly when Andrew Carnegie offered to give the *last* $50,000.[71]

The revelations from 1904 helped to get national legislation in 1907 prohibiting contributions by corporations. In 1908, the Democratic platform in words reminiscent of Roosevelt's postscript demanded Federal legislation

> forever terminating the partnership which has existed between corporations of the country and the Republican party under expressed or implied agreement that in return for the contribution of great sums of money wherewith to purchase elections, they should be allowed to continue substantially unmolested in their efforts to encroach upon the rights of the people.

The platform recited findings in the insurance investigation and Harriman's "open admission." The Democrats condemned the Republicans for failure to pass a law compelling publication of names of contributors and the amounts contributed. The Democrats likewise pledged themselves to pass such legislation including an individual "reasonable" maximum and publication before elections.[75]

Taft and Bryan in 1908 reached an agreement upon publication, but Taft refused to adopt publication before the election.[76] Interestingly, the man who had played a most important role as a collector of funds in Republican campaigns of 1868 and 1872, William E. Chandler, was a member of the committee which led the movement for publicity of campaign contributions. He declared the action of corporation officers to be "embezzlements of the corporation funds." [39]

Sensitive to the charges concerning 1904, Roosevelt wrote the Republican campaign chairman in 1908 requesting that no contributions be asked of Harriman and Archbold. He protested against any contributions from anyone who was being prosecuted by the national government. He cited his 1904 letter refusing a gift from Standard Oil Company. Boldly the President declared:

> I would rather see us defeated than receive one dollar from the sources I have mentioned. . . . The acceptance of a dollar from such a source would do more to hurt Mr. Taft than all the money you could collect would help him.[77]

Taft had already instructed Sheldon not to take money from trusts or people identified with them. Sheldon replied, "Will you please tell me, Mr. Secretary, where I am going to get the money?" He wanted to go to what Taft called "a narrow strip of street in New York." [77]

President Roosevelt and Bryan engaged in an interchange of acrimonious letters discussing the merits and demerits of individuals alleged to be connected with monopolies[71] as well as Roosevelt's opposition to prior publication of campaign contributions.

Suffice it to say that Taft recommended and Congress adopted in 1911 a national publicity law requiring the treasurer of every political committee to file with the clerk of the House of Representatives thirty days after election, an itemized statement of all receipts and expenditures, but no provision was made for the expenses of candidates.[76] This law was all the advocates of publicity had asked for.[39] It was in part, at least, the result of the Democratic triumph in the congressional election of 1910.[78]

Notwithstanding the passage of new legislation, the matter of money in politics continued to be important in the campaign of 1912. Aside from the attack of the Progressives upon the Taft administration for the Ballinger-Pinchot episode, the attempt of Theodore Roosevelt to set up a third party was vitiated by the presence of George W. Perkins, a Wall Street Morgan partner as chairman of the Progressive National Committee.[80] In fact, Perkins wrote the Trust plank and his threat to bolt the party caused Roosevelt to kill an offending provision. Indeed, some wealthy Progressives had originally supported LaFollette but withdrew their financial aid and gave it to Roosevelt. Roosevelt was sensitive to the problem of funds at the beginning of the race, saying that $500,000 would nominate LaFollette.[79] One of the decisive factors in defeating LaFollette's nomination and turning the tide to Roosevelt with the inevitable split in the Republican party insuring Wilson's election, was the withdrawal of "liberal" Republican money from LaFollette and giving it to Roosevelt.[80] Per-

kins and Munsey had financed Roosevelt aided by Mark
Hanna's son, Medill McCormick, and T. Coleman DuPont
among others. One account states they raised a million
dollars for Roosevelt's prenomination campaign.[80] Nonetheless, the Progressive platform pledged the party to
legislation compelling a "strict limitation of all campaign
contributions and expenditures, and detailed publicity of
both before as well as after primaries and elections." [75]

The Republicans favored additional legislation as necessary to prohibit corporations from contributing to campaigns for nomination or election of federal officials and
heartily approved of the act of Congress providing for "fullest" publicity on nominations and elections.[75] The Democrats agreed on prohibiting corporations from giving and
"any individual from contributing any amount above a
'reasonable maximum.' " [75]

Democrats also had financial problems in 1912. The re-
marks of one contributor are significant.

> I then agreed to subscribe a substantial sum, and, also, to
> undertake raising money from others. I found the first by far
> the easier to make good. To redeem the second was a very
> different matter: my friends in the business world looked
> upon me almost as one who had lost his reason. "Why," they
> asked, "should any one who has property be willing to entrust
> the management of the United States to the Democratic
> Party? How can a reasonable man hope for Wilson's nomina-
> tion against veterans like Bryan, Clark, and Underwood? And
> how can any Democrat hope for victory against the in-
> trenched Republicans?" It was the hardest proposition that
> I ever undertook to sell, but we *managed somehow to meet
> our financial emergencies as we came to them.*[81]

Wilson feared to enter politics because he was a poor
man unable to afford the expenses of a political career.[82]
Originally promoted by Wall Street forces (George Harvey), Wilson's dramatic conversion to reform had cut him
off from these sources of funds. His pre-nomination campaign was constantly in difficulty because of lack of funds,
but Wilson's Princeton classmate, Cleveland Dodge, who

had been a great reliance of Wilson when he was president of Princeton was the largest contributor with a donation covering half of the first $35,000. Henry Morgenthau, Sr. and Charles R. Crane, who likewise gave to LaFollette, helped out. In all, Wilson received about $200,000.[83] Even Bryan's brother, though William Jennings was pledged to Clark, gave Wilson a contribution.[83]

Wilson accepted money from many sources and neither he nor his managers examined the list of contributors carefully. Wilson once said the bulk came from small contributors. This was not the fact. Publicity in June instead of October might have been embarrassing. His very meticulous biographer concludes:

> The fact remains, furthermore, that the Wilson pre-convention campaign was financed by a few leading bankers and manufacturers. It is fantastic, however, to assume that there is any sinister implication in this fact; Wilson, it should be emphasized, did insist upon drawing a line between the wealthy men from whom he would accept and would not accept support.

Though he received gifts from Dodge and Morgenthau,

> on the other hand, Wilson would not accept the contributions of Ryan and Hearst; to be sure, he rejected Ryan's proffered contribution chiefly because he thought that it would injure his chances for the nomination if it became known that he had accepted Ryan money, but he did at least reject it, while Harmon and Underwood did not. There is not the slightest evidence to indicate that either Wilson or McCombe made any political commitments in exchange for financial contributions, or that Wilson was subsequently influenced by his financial backers.[82]

During his fall campaign, Wilson insisted upon complete publicity of contributions. In asking Henry Morgenthau to accept the chairmanship of the Finance Committee, Wilson wrote:

> I shall insist that no contributions whatever be even indirectly accepted from any corporation. I want especial attention paid

to small contributors, and I want great care exercised over the way the money is spent. . . . one thing more. There are three rich men in the Democratic party whose political affiliations are so unworthy that I shall depend on you personally to see that none of their money is used in my campaign.[88]

Morgenthau instituted a budget system "for the first time in American political history" [81] and ended with a surplus. The total contributed was $1,110,952.25. Almost one-third came from contributors giving less than $100. Altogether 88,229 persons contributed. One Princeton classmate, who was connected with International Harvester, withdrew his gift lest it embarrass Wilson.[83] Small donations were solicited in special campaigns. Great "dollar drives" were made and appeals sent to the voters telling them that Wilson was the people's candidate. Yet the conclusion of a careful scholar is:

> When one considers the really tremendous effort made by the Democratic newspapers to make the campaign fund drive a truly popular affair, it must be concluded that the mass appeal was a disappointing failure. The campaign of 1912, in short, was not financed by small contributions and had the campaign committee depended upon "the people" for financial support, the party would have been bankrupt indeed in November.[84]

Meanwhile, Roosevelt was embarrassed by Perkins, and Taft's erstwhile friends deserted him. Henry Clay Frick declared that he "would contribute almost any amount to insure the success of the Republican party if I thought it had a chance." Moreover, he did not care to contribute to this campaign because "the administration has utterly failed to treat many of its warmest friends fairly." [85] The steel magnate was offended because of charges made against him in an anti-trust suit. He concluded:

> The President, I think, also told me that he did not know that such a charge in the suit was to be made against me. This shows a great lack of interest in very important matters on the part of the President and his Secretary, Mr. Knox.

I write you this fully as I do not want my position mis-
understood.[85]

Employment of the sovereignty of the state against
economic combination had produced a response with the
power available in the arsenal of the economy.

In the reform legislation of the New Freedom nothing
was added directly with respect to politics and money,
though the Clayton Anti-Trust Act, the Underwood
Tariff law, and the Federal Reserve System readjusted the
previous balance of economic and political power, and the
Federal Trade Commission Act furthered the regulation of
business providing a basis of later significant connections.
Finally, the enactment of two constitutional amendments,
one for the direct taxation of income, paved the way for
one of the most important relationships of party finance in
subsequent decades; the other, the seventeenth amendment,
which provided for direct election of United States senators,
moved the choice of senators to the voters directly, frequently with nominations in costly direct primaries.

III

The United States Experience: Since 1916

Though campaign finance was not a prominent issue in 1916, as it had been for over twenty years, there were some interesting developments. The second largest Democratic contributor was E. L. Doheny,[1] who later won notoriety in the Teapot Dome oil scandal in the Harding administration. Doheny recouped his $50,000 by winning $300,000 on Wilson's close victory.[2] This large donation by a rich speculator was matched by a $1,000 contribution out of his personal savings by Franklin K. Lane, Secretary of the Interior. However, Morgenthau, now Ambassador to Turkey, started the financial campaign for a Democratic congress by underwriting a "modest" minimum sum. According to his report:

> This action greatly changed the attitude of the congressmen when they realized that help was at hand to make a real fight for the election. It practically created several hundred active campaign managers at a stroke.[3]

Another wealthy contributor was Henry Ford, but the canny automobile manufacturer received a *quid pro quo*.

Morgenthau's description shows an illuminating episode in fund collecting:

> He would contribute, but he wanted terms that would advertise himself and his cars. The advertisements, when published, must be in the form of a statement of Ford's personal views on the campaign, and must bear his signature. In addition, as compensation, we were to guarantee him the privilege of calling upon the President, so that he might lay before him the plan which he contemplated of adding the women in his employ to the men who were already benefitting by the minimum wage of $5 a day. He wanted the President, he said, to get the credit for advising him to make this arrangement. No doubt, he was even more anxious to get the publicity that would come from making the announcement after the visit.
>
> We accepted Ford's proposition, but he drove a hard bargain, for, after all, his contribution was a small one, and absurdly disproportionate to his means and to his professions of interest in the election.[2]

The end of the war period was marked by the extensive use of funds in a senatorial contest of wide importance. Theodore Roosevelt's former Secretary of the Navy, Truman H. Newberry, locked in a bitter contest for Republican nomination with Henry Ford, spent far in excess of the legal limit to achieve his victory. Seated by his peers in the Senate, his choice gave the Republicans the margin of one necessary to control the organization of that body. This majority of one gave Henry Cabot Lodge the chairmanship of the Senate Foreign Relations Committee. Political science has no answer to what the history of the next half century might have been if the Democrats had unseated Newberry in 1919, instead of 1922 when he resigned because so many Republican senators were defeated in primaries where Newberry's choice was an issue.[3]

Newberry's subsequent conviction for violation of the Corrupt Practices Act and the later invalidation[4] of so much of the Act as applied to primaries was the prelude to the 1920's with unlimited primary spending, many investigations, blasted political careers, efforts at objective study, and passage of some legislation.

The 1920 presidential nomination campaign was wide open. The two front runners spent large sums, especially General Leonard Wood, whose campaign manager was Colonel Procter, president of a soap factory. The nearly $2,000,000 spent by Wood's managers appeared large, but in view of an electorate now doubled by woman suffrage, was not too much greater proportionately than that spent by Roosevelt in 1912. Frank Lowden's cause was handicapped by the fact that his father-in-law was a Pullman, hence, the taint of wealth was upon him. His campaign was chiefly financed by his wife.[5]

Two delegates were allegedly bought in Missouri, thereby placing the mark of "fraud" upon Lowden. The Illinoisan was the victim of a combination of an inept campaign manager who sent money carelessly to Missouri politicians and a hostile congressional investigating committee which divulged this information just before the Republican convention opened.[5] It is dubious whether full publicity produced a wholesome result.[6] Herbert Hoover thought Lowden should have been nominated.[7] Lowden himself thought "the real cause of my defeat was probably the Missouri revelation."[5]

At any rate, the money charge seems to have been one of the decisive factors in the defeat of the leaders, resulting in the choice of Harding as a Dark Horse.

The dying Boise Penrose who had held on to the Republican organization in 1912 played a significant part in the choice.[8] Harding, the candidate who spent the smallest sum, was nominated.[9] Too much money could be dangerous to a candidacy.[10] Was this the result of the investigation into spending pushed by Senator Borah? What was desirable? Did publicity result in picking the best President? The fact that the leading candidates did not win partly because of the taint of money did not mean that money did not exert an influence in the result. One delegate wrote subsequently:

I have never seen a convention—and I have watched most of them since McKinley's first nomination—so completely dominated by sinister predatory economic forces as was this. It was controlled by a national committee representing plutocracy and United States senators, the political representatives of what Theodore Roosevelt had called amalgamated wealth. . . . Every delegation that I knew much about was loaded with one, two, or half a dozen representatives of national commodity interests—oil, railroads, telephones, steel, coal, and textiles.[11]

In the light of nearly forty years' developments would not the Illinois governor, or even the ambitious general, have saved both his party and his country much grief? The sequel to Harding's nomination and election need not be repeated.

During the ensuing campaign, the Republican chairman, Will H. Hays, tried to limit the amount of individual contributions in order to "clean up" politics.

I planned to raise a campaign fund that would keep the party free from obligation to any private interests or any rich men. So far as the Republicans were concerned, I was determined, in every possible way, to clean up politics.[12]

He discussed with the Democrats an arrangement to accept no gift above $1,000 with an expected party total of $2,000,000. If one thousand dollar gifts would not work possibly the limit could be raised to $5,000.

Nonetheless Democratic nominee Cox charged that $30,000,000 was being collected by the Republicans. Hays contends that this charge followed the failure of some wealthy men who had contributed to the Democrats in 1916, to do so in 1920. The 1916 Wilson fund, says Hays, had been $2,000,000 with a deficit of $600,000. In August 1920, the Democrats had collected only $100,000 and their campaign was about to fail while the Republicans had a published budget of $3,076,000. There were 12,389 individual contributors averaging $88.11 each. Just a few were over $1,000 and none over $2,500. These statements of Hays were published thirty-five years after the event.[12] Hays quoted with approval the comment of the Democratic National Chairman, Homer S. Cummings:

> "The real trouble with campaigns is not what the National Committee does, but what the independent, cooperating organizations which are not under proper control do. There the evil lies. The National Committee can't prevent it, but the government should. The law requires the national committee to make a sworn statement before and after election, but does not require this of other organizations. I think Mr. Hays and I would not disagree on this subject at all." [12]

This conclusion is significant in view of what the Hatch Act of twenty years later did, namely, disperse responsibility even more. Furthermore, Hays ignores in his *Memoirs* the relationship of Teapot Dome to the Republican campaign of 1920. A sophisticated editor who was a delegate to the Republican convention declared that it reeked of oil.[13] When Hays was called before an investigating committee his memory failed him. At first, he was "less than frank." He couldn't remember how much had come from Sinclair to make up the deficit. The total, he thought, was $75,000 of which $25,000 was returned. In trying to reconcile the differences, Hays "dodged, squirmed, quibbled" so that Alice Longworth wrote that Senator Walsh "practically tore [Hays] to pieces on the stand so thoroughly that it was unpleasant to watch." [14] Hays was at the time of the investigation "Czar" of the movies and remained so for many years. His job was to raise the moral tone of Hollywood. In later years, on the state level, a similar lapse of memory developed in a Democratic collector of campaign funds when he was cross-examined. The witness subsequently became a university vice president.[15]

Campaign funds were again a live political question in 1924, when the issue of "G.O.P. Corruption" was given first rank in the Democratic platform. The Democrats recommended positively, but rather vaguely:

> We demand that national elections shall hereafter be kept free from the poison of excessive private contributions. To

this end, we favor reasonable means of publicity, *at public expense,* so that candidates, properly before the people for federal offices, may present their claims at a minimum of cost. Such publicity should precede the primary and the election.

After adopting Theodore Roosevelt's suggestion of public payment, the Democrats reiterated their 1912 position and demanded a complete revision of the Corrupt Practices Act to prevent "Newberryism." [16]

Curiously enough LaFollette's platform had no specific discussion of the subject, and the Republicans did not repeat their prior pledges.[16]

Before the campaign had started, LaFollette had introduced a resolution to investigate expenditures in 1924, including money spent to defeat candidates as well as to elect them. Fairly early (October) in the campaign the president of the Pennsylvania Manufacturers Association declared:

> We have in LaFollette and Wheeler, a Lenine [sic] and Trotsky with a formidable band of followers made up of the vicious, ignorant and discontented element, openly organized for battle.[17]

LaFollette and Wheeler charged fifty cents and a dollar admission fees to their meetings and in addition passed the hat for funds. In one meeting 7500 persons paid one dollar each and in addition $1,000 was collected.[18]

The revelations of the Borah Committee inquiring into campaign funds were employed by LaFollette in his campaigning to show that a large part of a $437,000 fund had been used for "debunking LaFollette." Also, the publisher of the *Saturday Evening Post* was revealed to have spent $71,247 in newspaper "ads" in addition to $1,000 listed as a contribution. One advertisement (costing $40,221) called LaFollette the candidate of the "Reds, the Pinks, the Blues and the Yellows." The Wisconsin Progressive was frequently linked with the Reds, including a charge that Russian money had been sent through Mexico to aid the Progressives. Of the contributions to Republican funds, "75 per cent of the total sum reported has been contributed by officers or directors of corporations," while only two gifts of as much as $5,000 went to LaFollette.[17] One came from W. T. Raleigh, a manufacturer of patent medicine, who proffered as much as $40,000. The Republicans, according to the Borah report, had somewhat over $4,360,000 and the Democrats slightly over $820,000 while Progressives had almost $222,000, one-third from ticket and bond sales and half from contributors giving below $100 each. Coolidge had four times as much as his two opponents combined.[19]

The 1920's furnished additional fuel to the flames of public criticism of sources and amounts of campaign funds. First, however, Congress drew together sporadic legislative provisions into one consolidated and modified form. Primaries and conventions were expressly excluded from the Act to avoid the constitutional hazards of the Newberry decision. The act was broadened to cover "any committee, association, or organization which accepts contributions or makes expenditures for the purpose of influencing" . . . in two or more states, "if such committee . . . is a branch or subsidiary of a national committee, association or organization." The last provision was directed at the Anti-Saloon League and similar organizations,[20] operating as pressure groups. The adequacy of national legislation was brought into issue the following year, when in Illinois and Pennsylvania, the rivalry for two Senate seats produced enormous expenditures by all previous standards. In fact, two candidates in Illinois striving for the Republican senatorial nomination each spent twice as much as the total LaFollette and Wheeler outlay in the 1924 presidential campaign. The total of $972,925,[21] in fact, exceeded the entire amount spent by the Democratic party in the presidential campaign of 1924 and nearly equalled the entire expenditure of both Democrats and Progressives.

Not only the total amount but its source was the basis of criticism of Frank L. Smith. More than half of his contributions had come from public utility executives who had cases before the Illinois Commerce Commission, the body regulating utility rates in Illinois. Smith was its chairman. Samuel Insull had personally contributed at least $125,000. The money had been taken from the funds of his corporation, but he repaid the amount shortly after the investigation started. Smith was denied admission to the Senate when appointed to fill McKinley's unexpired term, and later to the term to which he had been elected though only his primary expenditures were in question. Finally, when he ran for renomination and election, he was twice rejected by the voters.[21]

In Pennsylvania, the Republican senatorial primary of 1926 resulted in expenditures of well over two millions, more than half of what the Coolidge forces had spent nationally in 1924. These large expenditures tended to convince many people of the truth of the Guggenheim observation in 1906 that primaries could be bought as well as state legislators.[22]

The Senate barred Vare from membership in 1927. Vare's hope to reach the Senate with Hoover's support is usually assigned as a reason for this seasoned politician's final decision to give the votes from Pennsylvania to Hoover thereby insuring his nomination. Vare never took his seat but one who spent almost as much did. Mrs. McCormick, who defeated Smith in Illinois, likewise spent extensively.[20]

The presidential canvass of 1928 did not witness a costly prenomination campaign since both nominees were without substantial opposition. Mr. Hoover's managers rounded up delegates from the south in the usual fashion.[23]

Alfred E. Smith was apparently determined to have ample funds. He made the chairman of the Finance Committee of General Motors, the chairman of the Democratic National Committee. All in all, the Democrats had five millionaires as heads of its campaign activities. The Democrats talked of plenty of money, but notwithstanding their expert managers, they entered the campaign with a surplus of $200,000, and ended it with a deficit of $1,500,000.[23]

The Democrats spent in all $7,152,511.43 while the

Republican costs reached $9,433,604.30 with a surplus of $600,000 left in the treasury.[23] This was the largest sum spent in American political history.[23] Two-thirds of the total came from gifts below $5,000 with the remainder in larger amounts. Their largest gift, the only one above $100,000, was $172,000. Forty-three per cent of the Democratic gifts came from below $5,000 and one-third above, as with the Republicans. They had three gifts of above $100,000.[23] The Republican platform in 1928 declared:

> The improper use of money in governmental and political affairs is a great national evil. One of the most effective remedies for this abuse is publicity in all matters touching campaign contributions and expenditures.[23]

The Democrats in similar language stated:

> We condemn the improper and excessive use of money in elections as a danger threatening the very existence of Democratic institutions. Republican expenditures in senatorial primaries and elections have been so exorbitant as to constitute a national scandal.

The Democrats, likewise, favored publicity and in identical language with Republicans pledged publication of full information on all financial matters beginning in August and each thirty days following.[23] The Republicans also pledged no deficit.

Notwithstanding the declared intentions of the parties, problems did arise, especially from the spending of funds by religious groups, ostensibly in support of the eighteenth amendment. Bishop James Cannon was very active in opposing Smith in Virginia. A single New York man of wealth had contributed $65,000 to Bishop Cannon with as much as $10,000 in cash. No one was able to determine where $48,000 of the Bishop's collection was spent. Cannon was able to defy a congressional committee investigating lobbying and campaign funds. Ultimately, another investigating committee showed that Bishop Cannon had received as much as $130,000 and revealed that he had not filed a full report as required by the Corrupt Practices Act. Finally in 1934, Cannon and his secretary were tried on a charge of conspiring to violate the Corrupt Practices Act. Both testified that his secretary knew nothing of the sums given by the New York philanthropist. This made a "conspiracy" conviction impossible, hence the jury found the pair not guilty.[24] This setback left the Corrupt Practices Act in a weakened position.

Likewise the development of a near dictatorship in one of the states during the late twenties and early thirties demonstrated the effectiveness of the use of state employees of the welfare, educational, and highway departments in the organization of political power.[25] The economic depression had shaken the country to its foundation and the question of unemployment had become foremost by 1932.

The 1930's not only saw a sharp curtailment of the amounts expended by parties but saw the entrance of labor unions as major contributors. Both parties in 1932 started with large contributors in charge of their finances. In fact, Raskob and his lieutenant, Jouett Shouse, operated the Democratic party under a kind of financial receivership for four years. The Democrats kept up a steady drumfire on the Hoover administration. This set a precedent for continuous opposition, party criticism, or "education" which might well become a part of the American two party system, if adequately financed. However, Raskob and Shouse felt themselves entitled to dominate the policies and personnel of the party and to select Smith as the nominee again. This group was opposed to the Democrats taking a "radical" line in policy.[26]

When Franklin D. Roosevelt's prospects were at a low ebb in May 1932, Mrs. Sara Delano Roosevelt was called upon to help out financially again.[27] Aware of the depression, she was cautious.[28]

Though expenses were reduced,[29] radio came into its own in 1932. One source estimated $5,000,000 spent on radio time alone, about one-fourth on nationwide hookups. The devices of salesmanship were being employed in politics. Radio was used by Roosevelt to offset the Republican preponderance of the press.[30] Bernard M. Baruch, a Democratic "angel," preferred to donate to senators personally but gave to others as well.[31]

The intervention of the Federal government into economic affairs both in public works programs and by relief projects made millions of industrially employed directly or indirectly employees of the state. Moreover, the direct efforts of the New Deal to encourage the organization of workers presented an entirely new situation. In 1936, labor organizations for the first time became significant contributors to national funds. John L. Lewis as head of the Committee for Industrial Organization came directly to the White House with a check for $250,000 and a photographer. A leading Roosevelt biographer writes:

> Roosevelt was all smiles, but he could not take the check. "No, John," he said. "Just keep it, and I'll call on you if and when any small need arises."
>
> Lewis left, grumbling that he had been outsmarted. He had been. During the next few weeks requests for money flowed in from Farley and from independent Roosevelt groups. In vain Lewis tried to stem the torrent by insisting on a written order from the President. Roosevelt backed up the requests with orders or with telephone calls. In the end Lewis's treasury was drained of almost half a million dollars—and without undue notice in the press.[32]

The consequences were considerable. The following year when Roosevelt proclaimed "a plague on both your houses," referring to capital and labor, Lewis was offended,[32] and in 1940 supported Willkie partly because he was unhappy over Roosevelt's ingratitude. Likewise, George L. Berry, who had headed the independent committee for Roosevelt in 1936 and had raised considerable sums, became the occasion for the breakup of the original Board of Directors of the Tennessee Valley Authority. Berry's exaggerated claims for damages induced by the destruction of his marble rights under one of the Authority's dams, at least raised the suspicion of fraud on the part of the Chairman.

When the Board disagreed over a procedure for handling the question a congressional investigation ensued.[33]

President Roosevelt continued to call upon John L. Lewis for financial help. During the "purge" primary campaign of 1938, Senator Barkley telephoned the President for help, and he in turn telephoned the United Mine Workers chief.[34]

At the same time Roosevelt, according to Ickes, offered as the "only reason he had not read him [Baruch] out of the Democratic party was because, like T. R., he hopes that a practical idealist like Baruch will help to finance Alben Barkley's campaign in Kentucky." [31]

The celebrated purge campaign of 1938, the boldest effort of a party leader to make over a political party's ideology into an image of that of its leader, was the occasion of a detailed and bitterly fought investigation of campaign methods by a congressional committee. A series of articles by a well known newspaper correspondent in a national chain of newspapers, hostile to Roosevelt, helped build the stereotype that the Works Progress Administration employees were being prostituted to the reelection of the Administration's senate majority leader.[35] The results of the primary and the later election did not sustain the charges.[36] Nonetheless, a national stereotype had been formed. Senator Hatch proposed legislation to outlaw political activity on the part of workers on the public payroll. His proposal was supported by Republicans and anti-New Deal Democrats. New Dealers were reluctant to support the measure.[37] When the act was finally passed with the unenthusiastic support of both Democrats and Republicans, the President considered a veto. His assistants prepared a possible veto message described by Ickes as a "brilliant piece of work."

> The theory of it was that the Hatch bill should be vetoed and that a much more comprehensive bill should be passed, one which would keep out of active Federal political participation not only Federal but state and county employees.[31]

There was evidence to the effect that the Act was sponsored by Vice President Garner with the intent of crippling the New Deal wing of the Democratic party in the struggle for control of the party in the 1940 presidential convention.[38] President Roosevelt approved the bill with a message stating his views on its limitations and suggesting a similar limitation upon state and local employees.[39] A second Hatch Act was enacted in 1940 applying similar prohibitions against political activity by employees of state agencies "financed in whole or in part by loans or grants made by the United States or any Federal agency." In addition amendments were offered by administration Democrats to fix a ceiling of $3,000,000 upon party expenses and a maximum of $5,000 for any one contributor.[40]

"I supported a move to limit campaign gifts to five thousand dollars—a rule which should be strictly enforced." [37] Senator Truman's primary costs in 1940 were to be slightly over $21,000. "Of this, $17,887.87 was donated to the campaign, and I had to bear the balance of $3,685.89 myself. There had been 1,026 contributors in all." [37]

Others than Senator Truman feared that the Hatch Act would weaken Federal political organization and strengthen state ones.[41]

The cumulative effect of the two Hatch Acts has been to reduce the power of United States senators and increase that of governors. In many states the governors can use the state employee, generally outside a civil service or "merit" system, to organize a party "machine" and determine the choice of presidential delegates to nominating conventions.[42] This is undoubtedly a major factor in the voluntary retirement of some Senators who sought election to governorships before 1960.[43] Certainly the power of the governors had a great deal to do with nominating Eisenhower in 1952 over Taft. The Senator had national committee support and a large senatorial following, but Governors Dewey, Warren, and Fine (Pennsylvania) were vastly more powerful. Thus, as a by-product of attempting to curb Federal employees and money in the political process, some rather unexpected developments have been produced.

The growing power of organized labor has disturbed both

Republicans and Southern Democrats. The organization of the Political Action Committee as its political arm by the CIO in the 1940's offered a threat of a potential labor party or a Democratic party dependent upon organized labor for funds as well as for votes. Suffice it to say that in passing the Smith-Connally Act in 1943 over President Roosevelt's veto, Congress prohibited labor unions from contributing directly from union funds to the coffers of political parties. This Act was passed as a war-time measure. One of its purposes was to weaken Roosevelt and the New Deal in the forthcoming contest for a fourth term. The measure was politically interwoven with the extension of a simplified ballot so soldiers overseas could vote. The anti-Roosevelt group professed to fear control of the soldier vote by the administration in power.[44] This prohibition upon the use of union funds applied only to the national political organizations but several states have made similar restrictions. In Wisconsin, for example, the Catlin Act, passed in 1956, was regarded as a body blow by the dominant Republicans to a reviving Democratic party. Nevertheless, the Democratic nominee for the Senate won in 1957.[45]

In 1947, the Taft-Hartley Act took the step of making illegal contributions by unions directly to national political funds.[46]

In the meantime, a technique not unlike that employed by the National Bank in 1832 developed to whittle down the effectiveness of legal prohibitions against corporation contributions. The Democrats led the way in 1936 by soliciting and selling business advertising in their national convention book. By selling copies autographed by President Roosevelt for high prices they indirectly defeated the restriction on corporate contributions. The Republicans were correctly outraged by this avoidance of the Corrupt Practices Act. The Hatch Act outlawed this innovation. Likewise, the invention of party dinners at high prices a plate with profits going for campaign expenses was a Democratic discovery. Shrewdly handled this could be a device enabling the party in power, in effect, to assess civil servants, especially those in the upper echelons where career promotions might be aided by presence at party dinners. Republicans have emulated this practice. Businessmen seeking government contracts in a time of war or great national defense effort when large sums of public funds are being spent may find it helpful to have some of their representatives present at party dinners, or at least to purchase tickets. This becomes a part of the highly developing art of "public relations."

In addition, corporations in Ohio in 1950, and in many other places later, utilized collateral advertising effectively. Senator Taft in 1950, and General Eisenhower in 1952, were emphasizing certain economic and political symbols such as "free enterprise," "big government," and similar generalities. Simultaneously businessmen and corporations spent large sums advertising the same symbols. In a period when taxes consume a large portion of income especially in the highest brackets, policy advertising may be employed as a means of creating "good will," thereby obtaining a deduction as a business expense. In so far as this lessens government income and necessitates collecting taxes from other sources, its effect is to create a government subsidy for promoting the interest of a particular party or group. Private utilities had engaged in this practice until the Internal Revenue Service, at the instigation of Senator Kefauver, ordered it to cease in 1958.

Labor, likewise, adopted the collateral approach. In Detroit as a part of its campaign of "education," the automobile union undertook to sponsor television programs introducing candidates who were friendly to labor. Whether this action is a violation of the Taft-Hartley Act is as yet undetermined by Supreme Court decision.

The presidential campaign of 1948 was notable for the unusual position of a President of the United States seeking reelection with so little money that his campaign almost collapsed. First, he had difficulty in obtaining anyone to manage his campaign finances.[47] The burden upon the finance chairman was enormous. He became personally responsible.

> On several occasions when the treasury of the committee was empty, [Louis] Johnson personally picked up the cost of operating the committee and meeting its payroll. He was repaid but this was not a measure of what he did in insuring continuity of operations.
>
> Johnson had a tremendous impact on the campaign. If it had not been for his truly Gargantuan fund-raising efforts, the whole thing would have collapsed. There would have been no money with which to pay for the President's campaign train; there'd have been no money for radio, no money for printing, no money for any of the multitude of items which require cash to be transformed into action.[47]

Independent Truman-Barkley Clubs were helpful by raising money and turning out advertising material.[47] Greek-Americans helped financially, on one occasion by collecting more than $25,000 in small amounts from Greek restaurants and businesses in New York City. This sum, brought to party headquarters in a paper shopping bag, was sufficient to save one more important broadcast.[47]

The Democrats even resorted to a week-end check exchange with their advertising agents to pay for one broadcast.[48] On another occasion, the President's campaign tour almost ended:

> Cash for the train had run out. It was an ignominious position for the President of the United States and for the Democratic Party. It seemed possible the entire party might have to alight and get back to Washington the best way they could.
>
> But this couldn't happen to Harry S. Truman, not in Oklahoma. Governor Turner and W. Elmer Harber of Shawnee, Oklahoma, held a collection party in the President's private car and raised enough cash to finance the rest of the current trip and, also, another cross-country trip.[47]

At one time, Truman was cut off the air by a radio company rule that any going over into another program required payment for the entire next period. An unsched-

uled statement to this effect by a party announcer produced
a number of small contributions.[47] Once Truman was re-
elected, funds came into the Democratic treasury in considerable amounts. Some checks were antedated and others
postdated. Many of the President's October opponents
showed up at his victory Jackson Day celebration.[49]

In 1952, considerable sums were spent in support of the
two chief contestants for the Republican nomination. In
Maine about $4,000 was spent by the Eisenhower forces.[50]
In New Hampshire, so important in launching of the Eisenhower candidacy and so significant in view of subsequent
developments, the Eisenhower managers were estimated to
have spent $65,000 to Taft's $50,000. Accusations of "political slush funds" were made on both sides.[50] The Texas
delegation was one of the decisive ones in the Republican
nominating convention. The contest for this delegation was
heated. The "visible" expenditures in advertising and campaigning generally indicated an "enormous" outlay. A
widely known columnist even estimated the sum spent by
the Eisenhower forces at between three and six million dollars.[51] In the Eisenhower delegation was the nationally ac-
claimed "wealthiest living American," an oil millionaire.
According to report he was one of the largest contributors
to the "party war chest." [51]

On the Pacific coast, the Oregon-for-Eisenhower committee reported receipts of $47,000 and expenses of $43,-
000. There were additional thousands spent.[52] In California,
the opponents of Governor Warren were estimated to have
spent between $500,000 and $600,000, though some people
thought it may have reached $1,000,000. Apparently it was
the "largest presidential campaign fund in California history." The successful Warren forces had expenditures of
much less, judged to be between $50,000 and $100,000
with some estimates as high as $150,000.[52]

In the midwest, the contests were less expensive, but in
Ohio the Taft organization was reported to have spent
$58,000 in the pre-primary campaign to Stassen's $4,485.[53]
In the small state of South Dakota, the expenditures of the

two chief candidates appear to have been nearly equal, with $44,000 for Eisenhower and $40,000 for Taft. The vote turned out almost as evenly with Taft barely winning.[53] Though there was no presidential primary in Michigan, in his Detroit appearance, General Eisenhower had the overt support of the automobile industry. At any rate, the Eisenhower adherents welcomed with pleasure the visit to the national convention of the leading executives of the two largest automobile manufacturers from Detroit.[53] The absence of a heated primary contest for the Democratic nomination left their nomination expenses less visible.

Television and the airplane came of age as political agencies in 1952. Both in the conventions and in the campaign which followed television played a significant if not major role in the outcome.[54]

The national sensation produced by revelations concerning vice presidential nominee Nixon's personal finances, including his special expense fund, dramatized the importance of money in a political career. Senator Nixon's effective defense would have been less potent in other media than television. The resulting publication of personal income tax data by several candidates demonstrated the relevancy of publicity of income tax returns.[55] The wide variety of groups supporting the two leading parties was much in evidence. The amount of money spent by the parties is uncertain. One report gives the total as $140,000,000.[56]

The increasing cost of campaigning is still a growing problem to political parties as is witnessed by the efforts to get widely based contributions in 1958, by an advertising campaign sponsored by a nonpartisan privately endowed foundation. Currently, the high cost of television campaigning has introduced a note of desperation into the activities of both parties. Republican women in 1958, actually appear to have considered the presentation of a strip-tease act as a method of collecting funds. During the congressional campaign of 1958, several developments indicated the volatile nature of campaign financing. First, in California the threat by one wing of the Republican party to cut off campaign funds at the source appeared to have been a major reason for the incumbent governor running for the senate instead of the governorship. As his chances of election dimmed, he moved closer to the opposing party thereby endangering the success of his own party.[57] Nationally, the party in power began raising fears of extremism from the opposition party to draw funds from its own right wing. According to report, sources usually available were failing to donate and were turning their resources over to extremist elements on the right acting as pressure groups.[58] At the same time, these groups were sponsoring anti-semitic, anti-Negro and other forms of "hate" propaganda in Wisconsin.[59] Moderation was not promoted by these tactics.

In Iowa, a past contribution to the campaign funds of the Democratic governor by the allegedly corrupt teamsters union was raised as a device for bringing him into disrepute on a "guilt by association" charge. Further, the advertising campaign of a state teachers association advocating the same policies as the Republican nominee was supporting was challenged by the governor as a partisan act threatening the non-taxable position of the association funds.[60]

A summary of the relation of money to politics in American political history shows no final answer to the question whether the economy controls the state or the state controls the economy. The very structure of the state (its civil service) was almost destroyed at one time by the conflict over economic policies. Generally, promoting a candidacy for the presidency has been as adventuresome as drilling for a "gusher" in oil. Occasionally, the same producers have undertaken both. Some candidates have been wealthy men (Tilden), others have depended upon a rich wife (Lowden), or a well-to-do mother (Franklin D. Roosevelt), or upon rich and ambitious friends (Cleveland and McKinley); still others have had a loyal and economically independent college classmate (Wilson), or have had the support of small organized groups of men and women of means. The factor of inherited wealth appears to be of increasing importance recently as is evident in the cases of such contemporaries as Harriman, Rockefeller, Kennedy, and Williams to mention a conspicuous few.

As long as both parties had substantial support from men of wealth, Cooke and Rothschild, for example, the two party system was not endangered. When credit (the gold standard) and accumulated wealth subsidized by tariffs or other indirect means are threatened by one party, as in the case of the Democrats (1896) and the Progressives (1912), the two party system may be placed in jeopardy for lack of a balanced presentation of differing points of view. The major national problem in the period was the control of economic monopoly. If action similar to that taken between 1932 and 1940 had been started in 1896, the entire nature of the present economy might well have been different. While wrestling with the issue of trust control, legislation regulating campaign funds was first passed, and such legislation still bears the earmarks of the epoch in which it was born. When the New Deal sharpened up the conflict between parties, new sources of financial support were essential to maintain the Democratic party, and since the Democrats had opened the way for the organization of trade unions, their fiscal aid to this party was to be expected. The legislation which cut off this source of supply was a severe blow, for with both organized labor and corporate capital neutralized legally together with federal governmental employees, the problem for party financial managers was well nigh insuperable. Meanwhile, technology and inflation had increased costs. When evidence was produced in the Kefauver investigation of crime that the underworld had become a source of support a shiver of fright went through many civic spines. It was time to look over the world for any available help or suggestions.

IV

The Norwegian Experience*

Perspective may be gained by a comparison and contrast with some other countries to see what, if any, light may be shed upon the factors entering into the problem. A vivid contrast may be obtained by examining political behavior in Norway, a small country with a population of three and one half million, but surely a political democracy by any classification.[1]

The original Norwegian constitution provided among the reasons for forfeiting the right to vote conviction "of having bought votes, sold his own vote, or voted in more than one Election Assembly." [2] This clause was not the result of any corrupt practices, but was copied from contemporary constitutions, for the problem of corrupt voting and fraud in elections has been and is today almost non-existent in Norway.[3]

* The greater portion of this chapter is based upon the author's personal interviews with prominent Norwegian politicians during the year 1954-55, while he was a Fulbright Research Scholar.

Since Norway became completely independent in 1905, no scandals have occurred in the operation of its electoral machinery. Honesty, therefore, is not a perennial issue in Norwegian elections. This is not the result of legal regulation for Norway has no legislation covering the topic of campaign funds.[4]

In respect to the issue of campaign funds, the Norwegian political atmosphere is remarkably free from rancor. None of the leaders of Norway's six parties accused the others of dishonesty.[5] Not even the Communist party leader charged the Labor party or the Conservatives with being dishonest or subverted by cash.[6] There were some rumors but no concrete evidence that the Norwegian Communist party received printing supplies from the Soviet Union.

However, adequate financing of political leaders and political parties has been a "grave" matter from the beginning.[7] Members of the Storting were paid sufficiently in the early years for the most numerous group, the farmers (Bonde), to pay their expenses and even save a little money. There were reports that the farmers engaged in—

> intrigue among them to be elected for the sake of the profit, to the exclusion of more able and educated men in the district,—clergy, public functionaries, or private gentlemen,— who would otherwise be preferred.[1]

The observer did not believe these reports, but thought payment of representatives helpful. He pointed out that there were representatives of other classes than the farmers. Political leadership was not profitable. Conservative party leaders scorned to take any pay in early days.[7]

Financial burdens hounded Johan Sverdrup, the great Liberal leader, who did so much to establish parliamentary government in Norway. He was constantly in debt, and his political duties prevented him from applying himself to his profession. Sums were collected for him in his middle years and at the time of his retirement when he was in his seventies.[8] Even though Sverdrup may have lacked a managerial sense with respect to money his situation was pitiable.[7]

In the twentieth century, when the shipowners were the dominant group in the Liberal party, the party had a succession of wealthy men as leaders while Conservative leaders were poor.[7] A literary figure like Carl J. Hambro found it difficult to maintain himself financially and still remain in politics. He often translated while seated in the Storting. Preoccupied with his work, he was often unprepared for debate and his effectiveness was lessened.[9] Finally, upon Hambro's retirement in 1958, he was unanimously voted a pension by the Storting upon the motion of a Labor leader and former prime minister.

In the early days of the Labor party, Labor members of the working class who were chosen to the Storting found the financial going difficult. Trade unions paid them salaries, but when defeated or not renominated their names might appear on charity lists.[7] Even now, Stortingsmen who are Laborites may be officials of trade union organizations or editors of party newspapers. Likewise, Conservatives may find sinecures on boards of directors of corporations, for the addition of one more "nincompoop" makes little difference.[10]

Labor has had three prime ministers since it came to power in 1935. All three have been poor men. The first one worked as a section hand on western railroads in the United States. When he retired, he was voted an honorary pension upon the motion of the Conservative leader.[11] Oscar Torp, when he resigned in 1955 as prime minister, became a county governor, one of the few patronage jobs in Norwegian politics. The present prime minister, Einar Gerhardsen, was first a newsboy and later a public employee in his early days. Afterward he became a trade union and party official. His property and income are limited.[12]

In most respects Norwegian parties and media of communication stand in sharp contrast to similar institutions in the United States. First of all, television did not exist before 1957. Radio and press are the chief media of party propaganda. The radio is a government owned monopoly operated on the model of the British Broadcasting Corporation, as "a State undertaking but is set up as an independent public legal entity." [13] There are no commercial or sponsored programs. The Board of Directors has a great deal of independence. The main purposes of the corporation are to "disseminate culture and education, and to promote good entertainment." The directors appear more interested in these features than in politics. Before the war there were very strict rules with respect to political broadcasts so they were almost completely omitted except for special speeches by party leaders during election campaigns. In recent years there is "a marked tendency towards bringing more politics to the microphone." [13]

During election campaigns each political party is allowed twenty minutes to present its case. The order of presentation is determined by drawing names from a hat. The parties follow each other on consecutive days. All parties participate in one two and one-half hour joint program.[14] All six parties have one representative, but in addition the "government," the party in power, has one representative. The parties themselves work out the rules.

The Norwegian radio broadcasts debates in the Storting but generally condenses the arguments. Some of these debates have extended for five and one-half hours but the time is generally reduced to one and one-half hours. Stortingsmen are apparently not completely satisfied, for once there was a proposal that a committee of four out of the Storting handle these programs but the Radio Corporation threatened to cut off the production altogether. This indicates remarkable independence in view of its dependence upon governmental subsidy. Questions asked in the Storting are edited so that those which are intended to attract political attention are eliminated.[15]

The Norwegian press is preeminently a party press. Out of 199 newspapers, 154 listed a political affiliation. Only five of the remaining 45 described themselves as "independent." [4] The press in Norway is of great importance politically both because editors play a leading role in na-

tional politics and because Norwegians are a literate people
with whom newspaper reading is a deeply rooted and
widespread habit. Moreover, book and pamphlet reading is
popular. Unaccustomed to the continuous and repetitive
efforts of commercial advertising through radio and television, Norwegians rely upon newspaper advertising but of
a less blatant type than in the United States.[16] In fact, it is
declared, "So far as is known, no other country possesses
so large a number of newspapers and specialized journals
per capita as Norway." [17]

One experienced Norwegian politician declared that as a
nation of newspaper readers, the Norwegian electorate is
too sophisticated for political demagoguery.[18] Some observers think that editors occupy a position in Norway
similar to that of lawyers in the American political system.

Competition to present ideas through the press is keen, so
much so that all parties strive to have organs in as many
localities as possible. The local party press is sometimes
subsidized by the profitable newspapers. Industry on occasion in the past has subsidized editors who presented a
point of view with which the industries sympathized.
This has not meant the editors were bought and paid for
since editors like to maintain their independence. The
grants to newspapers were more in the nature of subven-
tions given to men of talent by the great Whig landholders
in eighteenth century England. The contrast between
American and Norwegian press conditions is pointed up
by a Norwegian writer:

> Gradually, nearly all the more important dailies have become
> associated with political parties, a state of thing which, from
> a business point of view, is often somewhat unfortunate, as
> the big political parties believe it necessary to subsidize news-
> papers which would otherwise not be able financially to stand
> on their own feet. Moreover, these numerous "opinion" news-
> papers are forced to wage a stubborn war of competition, in
> order to get a fair share of the not too opulent advertising
> market. It may be mentioned that the labour press, though
> possessing a fair number of papers with a steady and rising

circulation, falls far short of the circulation of the non-social-ist press, which numbers, besides the country's two biggest papers, the leading papers in all the more populous provincial centres.[17]

The development of a Labor press was a principal factor in making possible, first, a successful trade union move-ment, and secondly, a cohesive Labor party. In fact, Labor party's "grand old man," Martin Tranmael, himself a long time editor of *Arbeiderbladet*, characterized the editorship of the paper as the most important or powerful position in the party—greater than that of party secretary and perhaps party leader. In this position the ideology of the masses was and is directed.[19] This party organ can speak for the Labor government, defend its policies and explain its purposes. The party has both an offensive and defensive weapon for daily advocacy of its point of view. A careful American scholar asserts:

> The Labor Party's principal asset is the well-developed labor press. There are forty-two daily or semiweekly labor news-papers in Norway, many of them the chief paper of the locality. In general, they are well edited, and provide a sufficiently rounded news service so that workers are not obliged to, and customarily do not read other newspapers, a practice which is fortified by the fact that almost the entire Norwegian press is avowedly political. Labor papers are usually owned by the local party organization, which elects the editor and determines policy.[20]

The Labor press is the point where the Labor party and trade unions merge into a solid front before industrial management. First of all, the Oslo paper, *Arbeiderbladet*, is profitable. It sells advertising to its adversaries, conserva-tive businessmen, who seek to obtain the wide market furnished by Labor readers. Indirectly, therefore, industry helps pay the costs of labor publicity. This item is of major importance in the struggle both for political and economic power. By consolidating its membership, indus-trial labor's consuming powers aid in promoting its polit-ical objectives.

It is noteworthy that the Communist party does not have a similar advantage.[6] In fact, no other party has this advantageous position. The trade unions took shares in a kind of holding company in which both party and unions join. It is extremely difficult to tell where union funds operate and where they leave off. One conservative complained that industrial peace—the absence of strikes—cut down on expenditures of union funds by labor, hence, increased their assets for political usage. The holding company is able to use its surplus to finance unprofitable papers in more remote areas. It is worth noting that the profit motive has not led to consolidation of newspapers as in the United States. Each party fears to eliminate its newspaper in a particular region lest the voters retaliate at the polls.[21] Hence, the competition in ideas and values is maintained from one year to another and not just in episodic publicity adventures whenever there is a biennial election. Also, the number of editors is larger. Though poorly paid, the presence of jobs for intellectuals enlarges the appeal of Labor to this important, if small, group in Norwegian society.[20]

The picture of the operations of the Labor party is singularly interesting in view of efforts to increase labor's political importance in the United States. To begin with, party and unions were inextricably interwoven in the beginning of both organizations. "The most prominent party leaders were also active trade unionists." [22]

In addition to income from the press, Norway's Labor party has had from the beginning (1887) income from collective affiliations of trade unions.[22] Also in the early days, a wealthy lawyer, a great idealist, who had "bells in his head," furnished money to help finance *Arbeiderbladet*.[8]

Today, there are large numbers of dues-paying members. For individuals this makes party membership a more meaningful enterprise since they invest in it. There are collective memberships as well. Unions pay membership fees for a certain number of members not necessarily the total of their union memberships. They have the "contracting out" system which means that social pressure is directed towards keeping all workers loyal to the Labor party. Not all union members do so, however. Certain unions contribute to the Communist party, for example, and sometimes contributions are made to other parties, but this is the exception rather than the rule. The system is rather complex with the majority in each of the local unions determining the amount and number of dues to be paid through collective affiliation. The funds are channeled upward through commune, district, and regional organizations with each unit in the party organization sharing in the funds.

Furthermore, there are youth and women's organizations which have dues-paying members. These groups play an important role in nominating candidates. Payment of party dues is a condition precedent to nomination for party candidature.[23] This requirement helps maintain party discipline and ideological unity. The Labor Prime Minister prefers the system of membership dues as a basis of party support. He deprecates lotteries.[24] Notwithstanding this disapproval in high quarters, the Labor party sets up lotteries with automobiles as the most frequent prizes. The income is considerable. Other parties are following the same practice.[21] In Denmark, the Social Democratic party owns a brewery and takes the profits from its beverage sales as a means to pay party expenses. Likewise, the same party operates a cooperative dairy.[25] Both Conservative and Labor party leaders think the other party has unlimited funds. This is probably a delusion.[26]

The Conservative party has the largest press support of the so-called "opposition" parties, but does not have the number of dues-paying members that Labor has.[27] The national party organization depends entirely upon individual gifts. Only a few contributors give as much as 5000 kroner (between $700 and $800). Most gifts range around 1000 kroner (around $150). Usually there are two or three thousand contributors, most of them businessmen, shipowners, and a few lawyers. Corporations as well as individuals donate. The absence of regular dues-paying members makes the amount of the budget uncertain. There are affiliated groups and local party units where dues are paid. In Oslo, there are 25,000 dues-paying members in the local organization. The dues are small—five kroner a year, about 75 cents.[28] Approximately 20,000 young people who belong to the Conservative young people's organization pay from three to six kroner a year dues.[29] The Conservative women's organization has 20,000 members who pay dues ranging from three to five kroner each.[30]

The Farmers' party was originally financed by the Farmers' Union which now functions independently of the party though there is a great deal of overlapping of leadership. All Stortingsmen of the Farmers' party are themselves farmers. The party has a body of dues-paying members who pay from five to twenty kroner a year. The dues are determined locally, hence vary from province to province. Fathers of families normally pay from ten to fifteen kroner a year and wives and grown children pay three to five kroner. Though dues payment is not required for participation in party meetings, no one will be nominated for office unless he pays his dues.[31]

The expenditures of the party are greater in election years than in "off" years. In 1953, the party spent less than $50,000. Slightly more than half of the off-year expenses came from party dues. With only one national paper which, though it operates independently of the party, supports in point of view, the Farmers' party does not have the advantage of a large press.

The other three parties are "poor" parties. The Christian Peoples' party has no national or regional press.[32] The party leader, himself a well-to-do lawyer, says his party has no money—is "very poor." [33] This is borne out by the party's income figures. In 1953, an election year, the party had 22,000 members who paid in slightly more than 65,000 kroner in all, or approximately 45 cents each. The following year with one thousand more members the income went up only 2500 kroner additional, or in all about $10,000.[34] The party leaders do not all share this poverty for two of the Christian Peoples' party's Stortingsmen are personally wealthy by Norwegian standards.[35] One of these was the only shipowner in the Storting, who had been a Liberal for fifty years and a very prominent official of its party organization. In his campaign he had the joint support of the Christian Peoples' party, the Liberals, and the Conservatives. His campaign was supported financially outside of the party's funds and without the knowledge of its officers.[36] The fact that the Christian party leader, a lawyer, has many shipowners as his clients led to the belief on the part of some Liberal party members that there was a financial link between the Christian party and the shipowners.[37] However, a representative of the shipping interests' public relations organization denied there was any direct fiscal connection with the Christian party's candidates, though there was an interest in the individual as a shipowner.[38]

The Norwegian Liberal party (Venestre), notwithstanding a great tradition, has no solid body of support in interest groups such as the farmers, trade unions and businessmen, or even of sentiment as is the case with the Christian Peoples' party. In accordance with party rules direct members of the Liberal organization must pay ten kroner dues annually. Between 1947 and 1951, the party's income had remained around 100,000 to 130,000 kroner (approximately $15,000 to $20,000) a year, with the exception of 1949, a Storting election year, when the sum was 267,639 kroner (under $40,000).[39] Its membership dues declined drastically from 80,556 kroner in 1947 to 8,344 kroner in 1950.[40] It is little wonder, therefore, that the youth organization of the Liberal party should have suggested public subventions for party financing.[41]

The Communist party is legal in Norway. Its representation in the Storting since the war has ranged from a maximum of 11 in 1945 to none in 1949. In 1953, the party elected 3 Stortingsmen but was reduced to 1 in 1957. The question of its financing is a matter of considerable attention in Norway and elsewhere. The evidence is elusive and contradictory. First, does the party receive funds or aid from the Soviet Union? The testimony of its leader was clear and direct. He denied emphatically that any aid came from outside Norway.[6] On the other hand rumor reported printing supplies (lead) and type were lent or given to the party paper, *Friheten*. Likewise disagreement exists as to whether any rich men ever contributed extensively to the party. Though vigorously denied by the leadership there is some very positive and reliable testimony to the contrary.[42] On the other hand, the small size of *Friheten* in comparison with that of the Labor and Conservative papers was pretty convincing that if any help was given it must have been small. The Communist organ apparently operates on a shoestring with a few very loyal members giving both of their means and labor.[43] The constitution of the Communist party provides for dues, collections, and party enterprises to raise funds. Failure of members to pay dues upon call, without valid reason, for three months, is cause for loss of membership.[44] Whether Communist Stortingsmen are compelled to contribute to the party is also in dispute.[45] The party makes reports of donations in its newspaper. According to these statements the larger part of Communist funds come from collections and rallies, including lotteries. Of the total income reported in 1951 (71,236.14 kroner) 57,419.92 kroner came from dues but other estimates indicate that about 200,000 kroner were received in support of *Friheten*.[46]

In conclusion, the available evidence indicates a cost of slightly over two kroner (30 cents) per Communist vote in the Storting election of 1949.[47] The Labor party spent about 32 cents for each vote received, the Farmers' party nearly 28 cents, the Conservative party approximately 65 cents, while the Liberals got a vote for each 16 cents and the Christian Peoples' party one for about 12 cents.[48]

The nature of the problem of party propaganda in Norway was brought into sharp focus by developments in the immediate postwar period. Large numbers of newspaper presses were destroyed during the war by enemy action. In the reconstruction period there was a certain competition among the parties to get their party organs restored to their former positions. Labor party adherents contend that their papers had suffered more at German hands. Conservatives argue that Swedish Social Democrats gave presses and other materials to the Labor party thereby giving an advantage to the leading party, and, moreover, the "government," that is, the Labor party, was favoring the reestablishment of Labor papers by import regulations and otherwise.[49] In 1947, a group of business people led by a prominent Oslo lawyer undertook to set up an organization by the name of *Libertas* (resembling somewhat in name and purpose the old Liberty League which operated in the first days of the New Deal) to collect funds from the shipowners and large-scale industrialists. By agreement of the parties each was to pay a certain sum in proportion to the tonnage operated by the firm or the amount of business turnover of an industry. These sums were to be allocated by Libertas to certain newspapers and to the Opposition parties to enable them to offset government propaganda and the work of the Labor newspapers. Libertas was originally a secret organization but according to its leaders, they intended to make public their activities after the organization was well established. Unfortunately for the purpose of the founders, news of its existence leaked out. The Labor paper, *Arbeiderbladet,* and *Dagbladet* (Venstre), attacked the new organization on the ground that its purposes were furtive and subterranean. A considerable flurry resulted with attacks and counterattacks.

It was as a result of this discussion that a Storting investigation was demanded, following a parliamentary interpellation, and a special committee was set up by the Storting to examine the whole question of campaign funds and their publicity. An attorney was appointed to aid the committee and a research organization was engaged to assist. Three years later the committee made its report recommending that no action be taken, not even providing for publicity of campaign contributions.[4]

Among other reasons for this position the committee stated that publication of the names of contributors would be a violation of the secrecy of the ballot, since it was assumed that contributors would vote for the party to which they contributed. This, of course, was not accurate in the case of Libertas which hoped to assist, and did aid, several Opposition parties. Libertas was compelled by the furor voluntarily to desist from its original purpose and cease contributions directly to the parties. Instead, it has become an independent business group for the purpose of "educating" the public on the nature of industry and management and generally supports the virtues of free enterprise. It may be pointed out that Conservative political leaders disliked to receive help from Libertas for they felt that funds which might come directly to the coffers of the party were diverted to this organization. The party leadership did not want to be dependent upon any single source for funds. In other words, politicians wanted freedom to determine their actions and policies without being the puppets of economic forces.

Another reason advanced by the committee for refusing to recommend any laws was that evasion of any statute which might be enacted would be too easy.

> It is in itself fairly unusual to make laws which are based on the belief that those the regulations are directed against will show good-will by complying with them, but without any possibility for the authorities to control so that the regulations are kept. Such legislation would not bind a party which did not find reason to exhibit loyalty towards the regulations of the law. And if legislation is slighted without the authorities having the opportunity to interfere, this can have the effect of breaking down respect for laws in a wider aspect.[4]

They were not impressed by American and British experience since conditions in these countries were not applicable in Norway.

Finally, the committee recommended that the parties voluntarily publish their financial records, but not include the names of contributors. In fact, all the parties agreed "in principle," in response to an inquiry, to cooperate in a voluntary arrangement.[4]

In 1955, the Storting accepted the committee report with a minimum of debate, less than an hour, in fact. No excitement marked the discussion. A mild smile greeted the observation of the Communist leader that the *Report* was a "stillborn mouse." [50]

Farmand, a journal generally critical of the Labor party, described the entire affair as "a singular fiasco" because it demonstrated the "demagogical methods used by that section of the Press." *Farmand* declared:

> However, neither the public nor the Commission of Enquiry took long to find out that an investigation into the non-socialist parties' finance would inevitably lead to an investigation into the Labour Party's finances as well. The Commission was composed of members of all parties, but its Report with this conclusion is unanimous. The Labour Party, having so to speak fallen into cold water, had to crawl out again, looking much the worse for its experience.[51]

In conclusion, this ardent advocate of free enterprise saw no need of secrecy:

> Why should anyone feel self-conscious about supporting views one believes to be the right ones? Or about supporting the political parties which stand for one's own political principles and ideas? We cannot even see anything particularly shocking in giving financial support to parties, whose interests are identical with one's own. Are not the workers and the trade unions doing just that? [51]

Libertas now maintains a short course school of "college" for education in business and economics. Its point of view is definitely anti-socialist.

Of collateral interest to a discussion of money in Norwegian politics is the fact that the definition of "political propaganda" is as difficult in Norway as in the United States and England. One of the Norwegian export firms carried a series of advertisements in two prominent, well established newspapers, *Morgenbladet* and *Aftenposten*. Short, pungent, and of an aphoristic nature, they were similar to the once popular Mr. Dooley and Will Rogers sayings. Frequently these advertisements directed critical comments towards the government, hinting at dictatorship.[52]

Both Liberal and Labor newspapers criticized the advertisements, declaring that such expenditures should be taxable under the income tax rather than deductible as business expenses. Shortly afterward an auditor from the Oslo tax office came to examine the company accounts. When asked why he was examining income rather than expenses, the auditor replied that he was looking for something paid from Libertas. The firm's representative declared that it had made no contributions to Libertas because no request had been made, but that the company was willing to do so.

A lawsuit followed over the taxability of expenses for advertising which was critical of public policy but was intended to create "good will." [53] The city challenged the business expenses argument contending that the advertisements were political in nature. One of those challenged marked election day in red letters but the company replied that it was not political to urge people to vote. The matter was tried in the courts and the company won both locally and nationally. The Supreme Court was unanimous in holding the advertisements to be outlays incurred for the purpose of earning income. The firm was allowed costs both in the lower and higher courts.[54]

A similar development has happened in countries which regulate money spent for political purposes as well. A famous case was that of "Mr. Cube," the advertisement carried in the British press by the sugar industry in opposition to the British Labour party's policy of proposed nationalization of sugar refining. The British courts upheld the right of a sugar refining corporation to spend money in this fashion, as justified expense in an effort to preserve the rights of property holders.[55]

In the United States both in the campaign of Senator Taft for reelection in 1950 and in the Eisenhower presidential campaign of 1952, widespread corporate and party advertising occurred simultaneously. The Republican party was emphasizing certain symbols of "free enterprise." The corporate advertisements did the same thing on a more abstract basis. Apparently this practice did not violate the Corrupt Practices Act nor did it prevent the corporations from deducting such expenses for income tax purposes.

In 1958, Senator Estes Kefauver obtained a ruling of the Internal Revenue Service that sums spent by private public utility companies in circulating propaganda against public ownership of utilities was not deductible as a legitimate business expense. Some newspapers are declaring this ruling a violation of freedom of the press.[56]

There are other features of Norwegian political life relating to the influence of money in politics. One factor of considerable significance in the absence of private enrichment at public expense may be the wide publicity of income and wealth statistics. Each year there is an assessment of both personal income and "fortune," or property ownership. These figures are open for public inspection for a few weeks during the month of August. More important yet, the figures for Oslo are privately published in a book which may be purchased at small cost.[57] Accordingly, any sudden increase in wealth would arouse suspicion and might lead to income tax prosecution. Only one state in the United States, Wisconsin, under the aegis of the LaFollettes, opened income tax returns to the public.[58]

An additional factor of significance in Norwegian, and for that matter in all Scandinavian politics, is the high percentage of voter participation.[59] Whether this is the result of a highly complex and intricate party organization or the cause of intense party activity is hard to determine. Certainly party life is more active and continuous, hence party membership is more organic than in a country where registration under the party name alone gives party membership, even though this does not mean the registrant votes the party ticket. Chiefly it means he can vote in a primary

for nominating candidates under the party name. The existence of the direct primary as a nominating device is an in-
stitutional difference between the United States and Norway which increases costs to candidates in America. The
fact that all expenses of running for public office are borne
either by the state or by the party immeasurably reduces
the fiscal burdens of holding public office. It probably also
serves to greatly strengthen party bonds.

The state in Norway has moved to the financial aid of
political parties in two ways, one direct and the other indirect. Norway adopted the American political convention
as a nominating device. The parties choose delegates in
communal conventions, but when the county or area convention meets the state pays the traveling and subsistence
expenses of the delegates.[60]

Finally, members of the Storting have a number of
privileges not given American congressmen. First, they are
entitled to free transportation on state railways, state-subsi-
dized ship lines and airlines. This makes it possible for a
party with a representation in the Storting to send its
membership into various election districts. The larger the
delegation the greater the opportunity for the party.
However, there is no evidence of widespread use of this
source of free travel.

Though the pay of a Stortingsman was not much larger
than the average income in 1955,[61] that is, 12,000 kroner
a year, yet together with the extra time, the pay ran to
about 21,000 kroner (about $3,000) of which two thirds
was tax-exempt.[62] Norwegian taxes are high and the
salary of Stortingsmen ranked well with that of an average
businessman. In 1958, salaries of Storting members were
raised to 20,000 kroner subject to both state and local
taxes. Replacing the old *per diem* is a cost of living supple-
ment varying from 9,000 kroner in Oslo to 12,600 kroner
for north Norway.[63]

Another matter of great importance is the fashion in
which national resources and credit have been treated in
Norway. Limited in resources and size Norwegians have

felt the necessity of exercising political control over economic growth.[64] The United States is still a young country. Government has had large natural resources to bestow upon the influential from the days of early settlement. Its vast natural wealth may have served to bring a closer irregular association between money and politics than in less favored areas where scarcity has to be evenly shared to permit survival. In Norway, important natural resources, especially water, remained state-owned or state-controlled, while public utilities, dependent upon water power, have been largely state-owned and state-operated. These are the sensitive zones where the influence of money has been most effective in politics in the United States. In Norway, technology has operated under collective control whereas in the United States and other western nations of larger size, technology under private control has been able to obtain powers rivaling those of the state in their effect as sanctions upon the state and the economy. Recently this has been vividly demonstrated in the media of communication where "natural" monopolies in radio and television are retained by the state as the agent of the people. In Norway, radio is not a tool to sell soap. It is not commercial but cultural; it is a medium of education and not of salesmanship. A realistic demonstration of American radio techniques caused educated Scandinavians to shudder.[65]

There is a further difference. In Norway, popular education preceded enfranchisement while in the United States the privilege of voting antedated education. In Norway, education came as a device to teach religion—the catechism. In addition, the folkschool movement which spread from Denmark has had a great influence in self-improvement of the underprivileged. This is shown in the large number of Labor party leaders who have worked up from the ranks through continuation schools.

Finally, the absence of extremes of wealth probably exerts a moderating influence in Norway. Writing of Australia almost forty years ago, that keen observer, James Bryce, noted that there are "few monopolists and no millionaires and nowhere else does wealth exert less influence upon legislation or administration." In a footnote he added that

> the only other democracies known to me in which money has counted so little in politics are the Orange Free State (as it was before the war of 1899), Switzerland and Norway, all of them countries in which there were hardly any considerable fortunes.[66]

Speaking admiringly of the Swiss, again he compared them with the Norwegians.

> There are no marked inequalities in wealth, and wealth, *per se,* is not an object of hatred. Its power is less felt in legislation than in any other modern country except Norway.[67]

V

New Directions

The basic problem of political leadership in representative government is to discover a means by which officials may be selected to act as the state's men (politicians) who will be aware of and sensitive to the various interests of a political society without being politically and personally dependent for livelihood upon private interests. Representatives need to be personally free of private economic compulsion in determining what they conceive to be the general interest. Representative government is a child of an agricultural society. For many years a governing elite of landed gentry with independent income served as the backbone of parliament in both England and the United States. In Norway self-sufficient farmers succeeded the original office-holding class. These men were a buffer between a growing corporate capitalism and a burgeoning urban mass. The Virginia elite from Washington to Harry Byrd, the New York patroons from Clinton to Franklin D. Roosevelt were in a position to be personally independent in their decisions upon affairs of state. In England, Gladstone, Disraeli (by marriage), and Churchill belonged to this governing class.

As agriculture succumbed to technology, the replacement of the leadership furnished by its independence has not been easy to find. Trade union leaders had no independent economic means. Payment from union funds left doubts as to the real responsibility of a Stortingsman or a member of the House of Commons. In Norway, Conservative leaders have shared poverty with Labor leaders. Businessmen were reluctant to heed even their own party leaders in pleas for greater financial rewards for those who give their services to political life.[1] However, Labor has been able to finance its party adequately enough for it to take over power and gradually to increase its proportion of the popular vote. Gradually the state has stepped in and provided salaries, as yet very inadequate in England, somewhat better in Norway and the United States. With the growth of the welfare state, pensions and social security have become part of the protection given to elected legislators as well as to bureaucracies, though American state legislatures have made less progress in this direction. Their pay is notoriously low, and they have the unfortunate reputation of being vulnerable to economic pressure.

However, higher pay and better pensions do not alone protect members of a representative assembly. The French National Assembly under the Fourth Republic was exposed to another source of danger. A highly disciplined party like the Communist party can use the state's money to advance its own propaganda. Members of the Communist party in France who were in the National Assembly agreed to have their salaries paid to a proxy who then turned them over into the coffers of the party. Leaders (in and outside of the Assembly) determined the amount to go to the respective Deputies. This is both the result of discipline and a weapon in maintaining discipline. With such iron control, power (sovereignty) may pass from the hands of the state's overt representative body into those of an outside party machine. The Communist party of France had the largest campaign funds of any of the parties in that multipartied country.[2]

Practices of a similar nature by which the funds of the state were used by a party developed in Italy where cities that fell under Communist control had the profits of their municipally owned utilities diverted into the treasury of the Communist party for organization and propaganda work.

The recent action of the Mississippi legislature appropriating a million dollars of state funds to the support of the white citizens councils of that state suggests the possibilities of the use of public funds for propaganda purposes to advance by publicly supported funds the interests of the dominant group in a commonwealth. The growth of ingenious devices for evasion of legal controls and the prospect of a monopoly of propaganda for a monolithic set of values is demonstrated by the suggestion of a left wing member (identified with the Bevanites) of the Labour party that confiscatory taxation by Socialists may be a means of depriving the Conservative party of its campaign funds.[3] The presence of high taxation was perhaps a factor in bringing the Conservative party in 1947 to a revision of its old policies of financing. Hitherto, according to a party official, the size of his financial donation determined the safety of the parliamentary seat allocated to him by the party managers.[4] Comparing the problem of party financing with the pre-war situation, the Conservatives officially state that "competition from the Socialists, anxious to repeat the victory of 1945, and with large contributions from the trade union and co-operative societies at their disposal is very strong indeed."[5] In its reorganization the Conservatives have sought a more broadly based financial support with thousands of dues-paying members. As the welfare state and war taxation move toward equalization of incomes, all modern democratic parties are compelled increasingly to turn to mass financial support or perish.

Finally, in this connection, it is important to point out the effectiveness of centrally controlled campaign funds as a device for party discipline. In Great Britain, the party leader, as prime minister, may subject uncooperative colleagues to the hazards of defeat or high costs of campaigning by dissolving parliament. With control over party finances the party leader may subject recalcitrants to withdrawal, or niggardly allocation of funds in case of uncooperative or independent action by individual members.

A critical reappraisal of the whole problem of money and the state is needed. First of all, the issue is not primarily a moral one. In one sense, the question is as non-moral as the transformation of static into kinetic energy. The question is whether a decision by voters actually reflects their views or whether the voters are simply a means of transmission of opinions manufactured for them and sold by a smaller and self-interested group. Here more information is needed about political behavior. It is easier to ask than to answer the question of why people vote or do not vote and why they vote one way or another. There is a considerable body of evidence to indicate that large numbers of voters, perhaps as many as 60% or 70%, always vote for the same party regardless of personalities or issues. However, sometimes a large enough group is willing to change its behavior, either by voting or not voting, or by switching from one party to the other that the amount of propaganda and the efficiency of the organization of one party over the other will be effective in determining the result. The more evenly divided the electorate is, the more important money probably is in effecting the outcome. It is safe to say that no amount of money the Republicans might have spent in 1932 and 1936 would have altered Roosevelt's triumphs. Eisenhower's two victories probably fall in the same category. The reelection of Wilson in 1916 and of Truman in 1948 are different matters. But in both campaigns the Republican party had more money but lost. Many other cases illustrate the same point. A similar assertion may be made with respect to results in one party states. No amount of money spent in Mississippi by Republicans or in Vermont by Democrats would shift the party voting allegiance. An economic depression or war is necessary to shake the voting habits of the traditional one party states. The Civil War and

its aftermath fixed the voting pattern of many of our
states so permanently that great emotional frustrations and
fears must be aroused to change them. It is dubious
whether campaign leaflets or speeches change many
opinions. Campaigning is chiefly a device for persuading
party members to get out and vote or get others to vote.

Probably circumstances beyond party control create fav-
orable or unfavorable attitudes toward one or the other
party before campaigns start. The accidents of events
such as the Suez outbreak in 1956 or the fall of France in
1940 are determinative for large blocks of voters. Long time
political education is of great importance. American parties
do little education between campaigns. They are very
inactive volcanoes. The party in power has a vast advantage especially in the presidency since the president is a
great source of news and no opposition leader can compare
with him in news value. Only two presidents have lost bids
for reelection since 1892, Taft and Hoover. One resulted
from a split party so that Taft could not have won regardless of the amount of money he spent in 1912. Hoover's
defeat in 1932 was determined by industrial depression.
In fact, only five other presidents in our history (the two
Adamses, Van Buren, Benjamin Harrison and Cleveland
once) have suffered defeats in seeking second terms. It
seems, therefore, that the great influence of money in the
United States is not between parties so much as within
parties in selecting candidates. Actually, it was the influence
of corporations over the nominating procedure which had
a great deal to do with the effort to control campaign funds
and take nominations away from delegates. LaFollette's
experience in Wisconsin, even though he was ultimately
nominated for governor by a convention, was influential in
developing party primaries. The role of money in the choice
of Harding in 1920, and its use by his unsuccessful opponents Lowden and Wood as well as the alleged purchase
of delegates to Republican conventions from the southern
states by Mark Hanna in 1896, and successively by Theodore Roosevelt and W. H. Taft by patronage in 1904, 1908,

and 1912, were prominent factors leading to movements away from the convention and in the direction of state control of the nominating process.

Likewise, one effect of "invisible government" in selecting nominees for senator and governor was to pave the way for further state intervention into the party process. The direct primary by requiring a second election has doubled the costs for candidates in two party states and occasionally in one party states. In one party states the primary became the election. However, a sitting senator or congressman has an enormous advantage over a newcomer unless there is some economic, social or political force which is undermining all incumbents. An incumbent normally can be relatively independent, for it requires more money to unseat him than to renominate and reelect him. This does not obscure the fact that running for public office is expensive but points up the conclusion that it is *not how much* but *how it is spent* that is important.

The direct purchase of votes, a long time practice, has declined. Newer safeguards in ballot preparation and electoral procedure, along with the widespread use of voting machines have made this kind of perversion of the electoral process difficult. The methods employed in purifying elections suggests the appropriation of public funds to improve the political process. Originally candidates and parties had to pay the costs of printing ballots and the expenses of election officers. Now the state generally provides ballots, or voting machines, and pays for holding elections. All of this was done for the purpose of insuring that votes actually reflected the judgments and beliefs of voters. In other words, the public will must be clear. The water of public opinion must run through clean conduits lest disease and dirt obstruct its passage. Yet a pure water supply demands more than sanitary pipes: water in an urban society must be cleansed by passing through many layers of sand to eliminate the original impurities before it enters the pipes for human consumption. This metaphor may be significant for a proper development of public opinion. An opinion, that is, a choice, without an understanding of the alternatives, without a comprehension of the facts which are available is not a real opinion. It is a stereotype based upon a pseudo-environment as Walter Lippmann termed it nearly forty years ago.

Thomas Jefferson intended the public schools to perform the function of creating rational opinions. John Stuart Mill declared that our masters, the newly enfranchised, must be educated. In an age of technology students of the public schools assert that not over 30% of entering students have the mental ability to comprehend the simplest processes of physical science. Politics is much more complex. Can teachers of social science ever develop a rational, much less a scientific approach to the limited areas in which facts can be produced? To ask the question is to receive a negative reply from thousands of teachers and professional politicians. Political parties, however, can simplify and sometimes oversimplify the issues before voters. Woodrow Wilson saw this clearly in the 1890's when he asserted:

> The arguments which induce popular action must always be broad and obvious arguments: only a very gross substance of concrete conception can make any impression on the minds of the masses; they must get their ideas very absolutely put, and are much readier to receive a half-truth which they can understand than a whole truth which has too many sides to be seen all at once.[6]

The first role of a political leader is to educate the people. Insofar as leaders clarify decisions and indicate the nature of choices before voters they are lifting masses of people to the highest level of thought to which they can reach— namely, to choose between two or more roads, to analyze two or more courses of action and decide which one they should follow. Dare the state leave this educational process to the voluntary efforts of political parties alone?

To do so is equivalent to cleansing the pipes but leaving the reservoir unattended. In a face to face rural or village society individuals may be able to judge the character of their fellows better than in a mass society where artifice becomes almost a science in itself and where the researches of psychology are constantly brought to bear upon the non-rational aspects of man's biologically inherited nature. A free society shudders at the controls exercised by totalitarian states in their need to manipulate the technocratic society. Can the free state advance the development of the rational in man by establishing certain procedures for purifying the source of public policy, that is, public opinion? The nearest to a human political laboratory in existence is the court procedure hammered out in the long process of history. The judge represents traditional procedures (law) and human impartiality raised to its highest degree. Rules of evidence restrict the testimony to the relevant and material and restrain consideration to the evidence—not to opinion.[7] The jury trial is not perfect, perhaps, frequently a tool for mistakes and miscarriages of justice, but it is a model of scientific precision compared with the normal American political campaign filled with charges and countercharges based upon rumor, distortion, and irrelevancy, not to mention falsehood. In England, heckling provides a certain check upon partisan oratory and tends to develop at least a minimum of rationality or cleverness in both candidate and voter.

One of the merits of the New England town meeting was that only those who listened to the argument were entitled to vote. American tradition gives an honorable position to public discussion and debate. The Federalist papers were fine examples of polemics addressed to man's reason. The Lincoln-Douglas debates of 1858 clarified the national atmosphere with respect to alternatives in the 1860 campaign. They made one of the debaters a national figure. In 1948, a debate between Thomas E. Dewey and Harold Stassen in Oregon was a major factor in Dewey's winning the primary and eventually the nomination.

The two party system can be to public policy what the adversary system is to justice. The presence of two trained professionals means that expert intelligence and competence will illuminate the matters at issue.

Jury trials are filled with drama. Plays and movies often make trials into best sellers. In pioneer days, lawyers won their reputations by their skill in trials where farmers and villagers could watch the adversaries develop their talents. One of the most challenging factors in a trial is the art of cross-examination. The skilled cross-examiner can easily break through opinion, hate, bias, and inaccuracy. The application of the jury trial procedure to politics would go a long way to destroy raw emotionalism and hysteria. If some mode of "due process of politics" could be introduced it would eliminate the worst features of campaigns like that waged against Senator Tydings in Maryland in 1950. The technique of McCarthyism, which was in effect listening only to the prosecutor's case, soon disappears when subjected to the corrosive acid of cross-examination.

America is currently going through a soul searching process to determine whether the virtues of the mind are to be rejuvenated. Party politics can be exciting, dramatic and mind challenging. The new media of radio and television are admirably adapted to bring the drama and excitement of politics into the homes of American voters and restore a sense of reality to so many who have sought escapism by creating fantasy worlds of entertainment as diversions. Rationality is man's chief defense against annihilation. Belief in rationality is the reason for permitting the free play of the mind. It is not enough for a state based upon freedom to adopt a *laissez faire* attitude towards the minds of voters. A negative view does not suffice. The positive view is indicated by the existence of the public school system itself. Millions are spent to train people for every vocation save that of politics. But a competent politics is the necessary means of survival of a free society. Is it too much to ask the state (taxpayers) to spend considerable sums to advance the art of politics both for leaders and voters? If this reasoning is sound, the approach to lessening the problems raised by the abuses of money in politics is for the state to furnish means by which parties and politicians can present their views of policy and value as well as their personalities before the voters in the best medium calculated to develop intelligence. This is no novel proposal. In fact, Theodore Roosevelt offered the idea more than a half century ago in an annual message to Congress. His full statement needs to be read.

> Under our form of government voting is not merely a right but a duty, and, moreover, a fundamental and necessary duty if a man is to be a good citizen. It is well to provide that corporations shall not contribute to Presidential or National campaigns, and furthermore to provide for the publication of both contributions and expenditures. There is, however, always danger in laws of this kind, which from their very nature are difficult of enforcement; the danger being lest they be obeyed only by the honest, and disobeyed by the unscrupulous, so as to act only as a penalty upon honest men. Moreover, no such law would hamper an unscrupulous man of unlimited means from buying his own way into office. There is a very radical measure which would, I believe, work a substantial improvement in our system of conducting a campaign, although I am well aware that it will take some time for people so to familiarize themselves with such a proposal as to be willing to consider its adoption. The need for collecting large campaign funds would vanish if Congress provided an appropriation for the proper and legitimate expenses of each of the great national parties, an appropriation ample enough to meet the necessity for thorough organization and machinery, which requires a large expenditure of money. Then the stipulation should be made that no party receiving campaign funds from the Treasury should accept more than a fixed amount from any individual subscriber or donor; and the necessary publicity for receipts and expenditures could without difficulty be provided.[8]

Five years later, when running for President as a Progressive, Roosevelt wrote privately:

> I am with you on the question of the State paying the election expenses right away now. I have always stood for that

course as the only one to give the poor man a fair chance in politics.[9]

When the case has been put so strongly the question arises, why has no action been taken? The reasons are several. First, how would amounts be rationed among the parties? Would each party receive the same amount? How about splinter parties? [10] This problem is almost identical to that of allocation of radio and television time in states where these media are owned by public corporations. In Great Britain the rule is to restrict time to the parties offering as many as fifty candidates. This is action designed to maintain the two party system and can possibly stand on its own merits.[11] There are probably other means of avoiding this dilemma. First, a public corporation can be created with representatives of both parties and a sufficient number of outstanding citizens composing the board of control which could administer the funds appropriated to it and make rules acceptable to the parties particularly interested. A second means is to allow the voters themselves to determine how their money shall be spent. The large number of income taxpayers suggests a method of achieving this end. Let Congress appropriate to political parties, for example, one dollar for each income-tax payer who is willing to signify the party of his choice. This could be done simply on a detachable coupon on each income tax return. There are between forty and fifty million taxpayers. Let us suppose that ten million people authorized a dollar to the Democrats and ten million to the Republicans. This would place each party on a permanent basis for operating each year. It could insure organization in each state of a party body seeking to advance the interest of an opposition party as well as the dominant party. Ultimately this might develop party organizations in each county in the United States. Support for permanent organizations certainly should enliven politics at the grass roots level and might eliminate one party counties which is something of a norm in American political life.

Undoubtedly the objection of too much power in the hands of the national and state party committees would be raised.[12] Perhaps the enhanced power in the party organization would induce closer harmony between party membership in Congress and the party outside. This reinforces the argument for a party council representative of elected party officials and of the party organization. The more parties become cohesive the more likely they are to be able to present coherent bodies of policy rather than have the drift which so frequently emerges from a temporary coalition of private interests. With budgets of ten millions of dollars the parties might be on a par with the better financed pressure groups. Undoubtedly, much more than these sums is spent by the interest groups operating separately.

The suggestion offered here does not contemplate compulsory giving to the parties. From the taxes of those taxpayers who do not choose to assign a dollar to their respective parties a similar sum could be appropriated to a public corporation set up as outlined above. This body might be called the Adult Political Education Corporation. The Corporation could receive gifts from private foundations or from individuals including sums for setting up an endowment. The purpose of the Corporation would be to stimulate public discussion, debate, and intelligent interest in public affairs. It might even sponsor "give-away" programs on the basis of knowledge of civic facts rather than the miscellany of isolated facts so popular on radio and television projects. A corporation with ten or twenty million a year at its command might go a long way in inventing imaginative means for eliminating some of the public apathy so prevalent with regard to political matters.

It is clear that smaller parties would have sums only in proportion to the number of income-tax payers willing to authorize their dollars to go to the lesser parties. This device would serve both as a barometer of taxpayer reaction and as an incentive for keeping the older parties abreast of popular feeling. A dramatic rise in funds for a third party would be a warning to the older parties to keep attuned to voter reactions.

The question of handling such funds in the nominating process offers complications but surely the payment of minimum sums towards defraying the expenses of delegates to national conventions would alleviate a condition where either the well-to-do or persons with "contacts" in unions or business are the most likely delegates. Selection as delegates could be opened to more persons of average means or less.

The party primary has a set of problems all of its own. Certainly the national party could appropriate some of its funds to be used in holding debates, discussions and round-tables among its adherents where candidates for nomination would have free time to display their personalities and policy suggestions before party followers. If the national party had a platform of policies, it might require as a condition of participation in these meetings an acceptance of party ideology. Undoubtedly there will be grave objection to this proposal from devotees of states' rights, but some unity of policy is necessary to national party cohesion. This might enable the parties to discourage some of the extremists who embarrass all parties on occasion.

Of course, this is a bare outline of what could be done. All novel suggestions are open to criticism as to detail of operation. This one is only meant to point a possible way over what has been regarded as an insuperable barrier to appropriation of public funds for party purposes. It goes without saying that as a condition of acceptance of such funds the parties would set up the best technical type of financial accounting and auditing of all funds with financial reports open to all parties, and to the press and other representatives of the media of communication. The present provisions for publicity do not guarantee publicity. A public corporation such as suggested here could buy time to report upon the financial activities of all parties, thereby ensuring the maximum of publicity rather than the present minimum.

Of course, there is the objection that this would constitute the use of public funds for political purposes. It is self-delusion to think that this is not the case now. Certainly the method outlined here is only to do directly and overtly what is now done indirectly and covertly. A good case can be made for the proposition that the sums spent in this manner would represent a very great reduction in the cost under the present arrangement to taxpayers and consumers. Parties might still collect additional sums but they would not be reduced to dire penury as is the case presently. The gain of confidence in our democratic political institutions could certainly represent an invisible asset of great proportions.

When new bodies of thought and new trends of belief unfold they are likely to make themselves manifest either by public propaganda or underground subversion. Jefferson's view that they should be in the open where reason can combat error still seems sound. Had not the unions been able to finance the Labor party in Norway the workers would have manifested their desires somehow, perhaps by revolution.[13]

In Russia, Lenin and Stalin so perverted ends to means that "forceful expropriation"—bank robbery in blunter parlance—was employed to get funds for the Bolshevik party.[14] Elaboration of comment upon such a dangerous course is scarcely necessary. Lenin probably used German money to advance the Russian Revolution in 1917. This illustrates the confusion of means and ends to which desperate and determined leaders may resort.[15]

Aside from the danger of subversion, there is another persuasive reason for public action. The unique position of the press whose freedom is guaranteed by the Constitution and whose income is underwritten in part by government in the form of low postage rates shows that adult civic education is already subsidized. Some well known chain publications receive almost as much in postal subsidies annually as might be appropriated to either of the major parties under the plan outlined here. In an age of technology, with a rapidly expanding and changing social order, it is doubtful whether leaving the chief channels of political power (parties) to the accident of financial benevolence or vested interest is a safe national policy.

Finally, inflation and other factors are narrowing the avenues of entry into the professions. The initial capital costs are so great that independent business opportunities are fewer. The farm no longer offers an outlet as the high price of land and of capital equipment lessens the prospects for independence in this traditional area of free enterprise. If, as seems likely, the doors to a political career are closed by growing expensiveness, the people and governmental services will suffer. A growing "alienation of choice," as the sociologists call it, may lead to further "fatalism of the multitude" as James Bryce described a mass tendency long ago.

The population of the United States will be 200,000,000 within a decade. Already 100,000,000 persons are eligible to vote. This is fifty times greater than the number when mass parties really started with John Quincy Adams and Andrew Jackson. Certainly the policies of the United States government are more than fifty times more complex. Technology will accelerate this complexity with more than arithmetical progression in the future. Surely an industrial society cannot afford to be self-conscious about everything but its politics. Opening the doors in politics to the best talent available does not seem unreasonable. The opportunities for rationalization of the policy making process are enormous and nowhere more so than in the region of money in national politics.

It is probably time for a reconsideration of the entire area of the state's relation to party. Inhibitions upon party conduct set up really to control corporations and subsequently expanded to regulate trade unions, need to be reevaluated to see if they are outmoded. If, as has been suggested, the American economy is one of countervailing power perhaps the opposing forces should be permitted to operate with greater freedom in politics.[16] If trade unions are able to offset the power of large units of capital by the concentration of large numbers of small sums, as has happened on a smaller scale in Norway and to an extent in Great Britain, there is little need to pass laws governing contributions of funds in a vain effort to regulate and thereby drive underground much of party activity. Outlawing so much of party work may make the entire party process seem unsavory.

A long time student of campaign finance has declared that the Hatch Act might correctly be called "an Act to Promote Pernicious Political Activities." She concludes,

> It defeats its own purpose by encouraging decentralization, evasion and concealment. Worst of all it makes difficult if not impossible that publicity which is essential to full understanding of who pays our political bills—and why.[17]

The Corrupt Practices Act appears ineffective in at least one of the states where regulation of campaign funds originally started. The use of voluntary committees has made a hollow shell of formal party structure and a mockery of legal limits on expenditures by candidates and formal party organizations.[18] Two-thirds of the states have passed legislation prohibiting corporations from contributing while one-sixth have placed similar restrictions upon trade unions. It would be worthwhile to compare the practices in states with and without such regulatory laws. Only one-fourth of the forty-eight states make it illegal to solicit campaign contributions from state employees.[19] In two of the states having such prohibitions the practice of collecting funds from employees is still rife according to reliable reports.[20]

Local and municipal employees are relatively unprotected, though cities are generally better off than counties. The situation existing in Kentucky today, both on state and county levels, was aptly described by Theodore Roosevelt more than sixty years ago when he wrote:

> There is no meaner species of swindling than to blackmail them [employees] for the sake of a political organization . . .
> Moreover, it is the poorest and most helpless class who

are most apt to be coerced into paying. . . . Another thing
to be kept in mind in dealing with these cases of political
blackmail, is that really but a comparatively small portion
of the funds obtained goes to the benefit of the party organization. A certain proportion gets lost in the transit, and
when the collecting officers and clubs are of low character
this proportion becomes very large indeed. The money that is
collected is used, in the great majority of cases, not to
further the welfare of the party as a whole, but to further
the designs of certain individuals in it, who are quite as willing to use the funds they have obtained against their factional
foes in their own organization as against the common party
foe without.[31]

In the light of this situation, substantiated by the critical
judgments of careful scholars as well as the fact that both
Norway and Sweden,[22] after thoughtful investigation, rejected any regulation of party finance, a long range reappraisal is in order. Denmark has not found it necessary
to investigate the feasibility of such action.[23] It would seem
both timely and appropriate for a body similar to the
Hoover Commission to make a survey resembling the *Report of the Broadcasting Committee,* 1949, in Great Britain.
The membership of the commission should include legislators, active and retired politicians, judges, and scholars
in political science and economics. Most, if not all, in-
quiries made prior to the present have been motivated in
great measure by the desire for partisan advantage.[24] Given
the power of subpoena a select committee might do for this
area of politics what the Temporary National Economic
Committee did for economics in 1938-39. A detailed
investigation on this scale should inquire into the relation
of legislation on campaign funds to the uniquely American
anti-trust policy.[25]

Another approach is the development of a dues-paying
membership in political parties, though this would only
solve part of the problem. As pointed out earlier, party
membership is meaningless in the United States. The suggestion that a voter should be a dues-paying member of a

political party before participating in its activities undoubtedly shocks the sense of the *natural right to vote* tradition so prevalent in American society. This same objection is not raised to membership in pressure groups, all of which have membership dues. It may be that payment of membership dues encourages interest in an organization, develops a sense of belonging, and of course, produces a participant rather than an observer attitude. Politics like sports may suffer with the spectator disease. Not observation but participation makes a dynamic citizenship.

Political parties need to reward participation and active membership. The Democrats, for example, could give one delegate to its national convention to each group of 10,000 dues-paying members. This, of course, should not be in addition to, but in substitution for a number of delegates now given on an area basis. If one delegate at large in a state were allowed to a group of party members who are militant enough to contribute five dollars as a minimum and twenty-five as a maximum, the party could build up a series of party branches with loyalty to an idea or a value instead of to a locality. This might go far towards producing a more dynamic party with policy interests. These party bodies, leagues, or functional groups could then express themselves through a political party instead of as a pressure group. Their pressure could be brought directly to bear upon party policy of a general nature rather than upon the legislators and administrators. Each one of these bodies could offer candidates for nomination within the party, whereby young people, women, farmers, consumers, workers, and businessmen might by helping to finance a party make themselves felt as a group of citizens holding similar policy views. A development of this kind would require relaxation of certain party controls set up by state statutes. In fact, the rules for the parties are so rigidly controlled by statute in some states that no flexibility is left. Indeed, the parties have been so formalized by legislation that they are agents of the state to nominate candidates rather than voluntary associations with their own rules and regulations.[26]

The 1958 campaign to get more contributions for parties had the earmarks of a community chest drive. For example, one corporation's executives set the tone by having the president give to the Democratic and the vice president to the Republican party. What would have been the case if all the top executives had belonged to one party? Will not the attitude of the higher rungs in the hierarchy govern those lower down? The fact that more than two-thirds of the company's employees gave an average of two dollars each does not set any precedent that such gifts will be continued. Though the corporation executives may have been moved by a sense of civic duty nothing in this conduct shows anything more than an ephemeral reaction to a national advertising campaign.[27] Did not this whole campaign with singing commercials and "hard sells" give an atmosphere of salesmanship to the serious business of statesmanship? Are there other means of achieving less expensive access to the popular media of communication?

There are various ways by which the end could be attained. First of all, the state can require the media of communication (radio and television) to furnish free time for the presentation of debate, cross-examination, and discussion. This would remove one of the chief reasons for the accumulation of campaign funds—namely, to purchase access to the voters. Secondly, the interest elicited by these public discussions would remove a considerable part of the expense of getting voters to come to the polls. A third possibility is to nationalize the natural monopolistic media (radio and television) as has been done in European countries, though as we have seen, no finally satisfactory solution has been reached in the matter of political propaganda. Fourth, there are private means of approaching the problem. Educational foundations, many of them avenues of escape from taxation, are spending large sums upon education, some of them upon adult education. Can they not by purchasing time for public debate, analysis, and presentation of party politics take a further and perhaps more meaningful step towards public enlightenment by furnishing the necessary time on the popular media for civic education? Of course, such grants should go only to politicians willing to subject themselves to Opposition debate and cross-examination by skilled technicians from many sides. Certainly the foundations would not be guilty of partisan conduct by offering free facilities to both parties or to all candidates? [28]

A compulsory vote law would likewise insure a large turnout of voters. Getting out the vote consumes a large part of the energy of the party organizations as well as their money.

Finally, the process of determining the facts in contested elections can be improved by transferring the finding of facts from legislatures to the judiciary.

A striking step was taken in Great Britain in 1883, when party contests were removed from party decisions and placed in judicial hands. The most vigorous sanctions ever placed upon excess expenditures in the United States was the denial of Senate seats to two men, Frank L. Smith, of Illinois, and Wiliam S. Vare, of Pennsylvania, because they had spent too much money in primaries. This action was accomplished by a coalition of the minority party with a rebellious group in the majority party. Ordinarily party discipline and personal self-interest govern decisions so that party contests are not settled upon their merits but upon a party basis. The establishment of an electoral court to hear disputed elections, make findings of facts, and report to legislative bodies might go far towards the elimination of irregular practices. Confidence in the electoral process could be greatly strengthened in this manner. The question arises how to set up such an important tribunal.

Retired members of the Supreme Court and other branches of the Federal judiciary could be assigned to such duties by the Chief Justice. Congress could give jurisdiction to such a court. If the court is established in advance, and its members should be disinterested, as would be the case with the retired judges, not too much difficulty should be incurred in gaining respect for its decisions. Likewise, in the case of party agreements, or intra-party codes, the limitations voluntarily arrived at could be handled by similar bodies within the parties. Certainly the credentials committees of nominating conventions settle disputes upon the basis of power rather than legality. The results of the Republican conventions of 1912 and 1952 were determined by the actions of their credentials committees. Internal party harmony might be promoted and the intensity of party dissension considerably reduced by producing a result in consonance with the facts. Party action by a numerical majority is inflamed frequently by emotion and distorted by interest.

In the final analysis one of the ultimate purposes of a free society is to build up confidence in its own procedures. If, as Aristotle suggested, the essence of statecraft is to maintain a differential equality, a balance between those who wish equality in everything and those who want inequality in everything, then the opportunity to express one's views, to present one's values to his fellow citizens, and to have been fully and fairly heard is all a free society can do. Today the problem of balance between private production and public services is critical.[29] Opportunity to present a wide variety of points of view upon the disposition of the new affluence is necessary in maintaining a nice proportion of values. Surely our politics can share in the new abundance as well as the economy unless the pessimistic prophecies voiced by Henry Adams fifty years ago are to become true.

> Our main difficulty is that our whole political system is helplessly cumbrous and antiquated and beyond patching. We can perhaps make it run your time, but, at the pace since mine began, it will break down like Russia within a perfectly visible date.[30]

NOTES

(To avoid giving a disproportionate amount of space to documentation in a study of this character, authorities are usually cited at length only once. Where further mention has been made, in the text, of the same source, the reference number given is that of the first citation.)

I   THE BROAD NATURE OF THE PROBLEM

1. Chang, Sherman, *The Marxian Theory of the State,* 1931, p. 46. Chang quotes Engels: "It (the state) is simply a product of society at a certain stage of evolution." Engels concludes: "and *this power,* the outgrowth of society, but assuming supremacy over it and becoming more and more divorced from it, *is the state.*" p. 47. Emphasis is Chang's.

2. See John Stuart Mill's statement: "Government is at once a great influence acting on the human mind, and a set of organised arrangements for public business: in the first capacity its beneficial action is chiefly indirect, but not therefore less vital, while its mischievous action may be direct." *Utilitarianism, Liberty, Representative Government,* Everyman Edition, 1931, p. 195.

II   THE UNITED STATES EXPERIENCE: TO 1916

1. Beard, Charles A., *Economic Origins of the Constitution of the United States,* 1929, p. 325. "The Constitution . . . was the work of a consolidated group whose interests knew no state boundaries and were truly national in their scope."

2. *Fletcher v. Peck*, 6 Cranch, 87 (1810).

3. This problem goes to the heart of political philosophy—Rousseau's general will and individual will: "It is ever the way of men to wish their own good, but they do not at all times see where that good lies. The People are never corrupted though often deceived, and it is only when they are deceived that they appear to will what is evil." Rousseau's *Social Contract*, Galaxy edition, 1949, p. 193. It is Plato's question of prudence versus justice. See also Dewey, John, *The Public and Its Problems*, 1927, p. 125.

4. Adams, Brooks, *A Theory of Social Revolution*, 1913, p. 209.

5. McLaughlin, A. C., *The Courts, the Constitution, and Parties*, 1912, Chap. II. "The Significance of Political Parties." ". . . the spoils system was a device whereby the party was provided with funds from the public treasury." P. 125.

6. Shachner, Nathan, *Thomas Jefferson*, II, 1951, p. 624.

7. *Ibid.*, p. 644. This was a "scurrilous" attack on Washington and Adams.

8. *Ibid.*, p. 889. Perhaps it was Jefferson's agricultural business —the operation of a plantation—not his expenses as President which brought him financial disaster: "not his expenses as President, but his expenses as planter dragged him down." Adams, Henry, *History of the United States During the Administration of Thomas Jefferson*, 1930, II, p. 470.

9. Dangerfield, George, *The Era of Good Feeling*, 1952.

10. Amos Kendall, Francis Blair, Isaac Hill and Duff Green. Public printing helped sustain them and could be a profitable business as well. The nation's first political boss found the job of printing in New York worth $30,000 a year in the 1830's. Van Deusen, Glynden G., *Thurlow Weed: Wizard of the Lobby*, 1947, pp. 107-8.

11. All figures in early elections and censuses have to be treated cautiously, but this figure represents the approximate proportion. Of course, many states changed from giving elec-

toral votes by the legislature to a popular basis. The number
of voters increased from 1,250,000 to over 2,000,000 and
the votes cast more than tripled from 352,062 in 1824, to
1,156,328 in 1828, or from 28.4% to 55.3% of white males
over 21.

12. *Memoirs of John Quincy Adams*, 1875, VII, pp. 468-470.
Entry of March 8, 1828.

13. *Webster manuscript*, Library of Congress, Clay to Webster.

14. Clay to Webster, Oct. 25, 1827. He mentioned Hammond
again.

15. A former student and a devoted follower of Clay's, at one
time United States Senator from Louisiana.

16. Five hundred fifty-eight dollars was spent for printing,
wrapping and distributing 30,000 copies of "General Jackson's veto." Gammon, Samuel Rhea, Jr., *The Presidential
Campaign of 1832*, Baltimore, 1922, p. 150.

17. *Ibid.*, p. 151. Gammon estimated that this would represent
half a million dollars in 1920. In the 1950's it would be
closer to a million.

18. Belmont, Perry, "Publicity of Election Expenditures," in
North American Review, CLXXX (1905), p. 167. The quo-
tation is from William Graham Sumner's *Life of Jackson*.

19. Van Deusen, Glynden G., *Thurlow Weed: Wizard of the
Lobby*, 1947, p. 108.

20. *Clay Mss.*, Library of Congress, Account of Hamilton,
Ohio, Whig meeting, January 1, 1844.

21. *Clay Mss.*, Library of Congress, *Bacon to Clay*, 1844.

22. Mueller, Henry R., *The Whig Party in Pennsylvania*, 1922,
p. 158. Footnote quoting letter from *Buchanan Mss.*

23. John M. Clayton to J. J. Crittenden, October 8, 1851, in
Coleman, Mrs. Chapman, *The Life of John J. Crittenden*,
1873, II, pp. 10-11. The irrepressible Clayton suggested that
Crittenden fortify himself with a bottle of whiskey before
discussing the matter with the President!

24. Nicholas, Roy Franklin, *The Democratic Machine 1850-1852*.

25. Belmont, Perry, *An American Democrat*, New York, 1940, p. 76.

26. Nicolay, John G. and John Hay, "Abraham Lincoln: A History," in *Century N. S.*, XI (1886-7), p. 522. Based on the recollections of Joshua Speed.

27. In *The Personal Finances of Abraham Lincoln*, 1943, p. 100, Harry E. Pratt states that it is highly improbable that Speed, Lincoln's friend and donor, was in Springfield in 1846, since he had left in 1841. Hay and Nicolay do not include this story in their biography.

28. See letters in Herndon's *Life of Lincoln*, 1930, pp. 328-329. The donor was an iron works manager who also took part in politics. Pratt, *op. cit.*, pp. 103-4.

29. Sandburg, Carl, *Abraham Lincoln*, II, pp. 167-8.

30. Beveridge, Albert J., *Abraham Lincoln*, IV, 1928, p. 335.

31. Herndon, *Life of Lincoln*, 1930, pp. 370-1.

32. *The Collected Works of Abraham Lincoln*, IV, p. 49. The recipient was described as "distressingly impecunious and awfully bibulous." Whitney, Henry C., *Life on the Circuit With Lincoln*, 1940, p. 333.

33. Harper, Robert S., *Lincoln and the Press*, 1951, pp. 76-77.

34. Sandburg, *op. cit.*, II, p. 342. The "price" almost lost the Union itself when Cameron's regime of war contracting resulted in inferior military equipment. Lincoln sent Cameron to Russia after "persuading" Cassius Clay that he was "expendable." See Thomas, Benjamin, *Abraham Lincoln*, 1952, p. 293, and Woldman, Albert A., *Lincoln and the Russians*, 1952, p. 114-123. Details may be found in Sandburg, *op. cit.*, III, pp. 422-454.

35. Belmont, Perry, "Publicity of Election Expenditures," *North American Review*, CLXXX (1905), p. 166.

36. Luthin, Reinhard, *First Lincoln Campaign*, 1944.

37. *Ibid.*, pp. 197-8. The italics are Luthin's.

38. Oberholtzer, Ellis Paxson, *Jay Cooke, Financier of the Civil War,* 1907.

39. Richardson, Leon Burr, *William E. Chandler: Republican,* New York, 1940.

40. Coleman, Charles H., *The Election of 1868,* 1933.

41. Oberholtzer, *United States,* 1926, Vol. II, p. 187.

42. Larson, Henrietta M., *Jay Cooke: Private Banker,* 1936. This biographer observes: "Jay Cooke and his partners had various means by which to keep in touch with Congress and to bring pressure to bear in their own favor. There was first and foremost the Washington brother, the official contact man and lobbyist for the Cookes. It is difficult to estimate the value of Henry Cooke to the group. Like the Rothschilds, he tried to stay close to men in power. He seems to have known everybody worth knowing; he entertained lavishly at his home; his office was almost like a political club. Needy congressmen sought loans at his bank—Jay Cooke and Company and the First National—and President Grant enjoyed many a cheering glass at his home." P. 200.

43. Bigelow, John, ed., *Letters and Literary Memorials of Samuel J. Tilden,* 1908, p. 245.

44. Flick, Alexander, *Samuel J. Tilden,* 1940, p. 303.

45. "The money was raised with great difficulty, so that Mr. Cooper and I, in addition to our personal subscriptions which were the largest ones made to the committee, were often in advance to a considerable amount. It is proper to add, however, that considerable sums of money were handed directly to Mr. Tilden and by him not handed over to the treasurer. Out of these funds thus placed under his personal control the expenses of the 'literary bureau' were defrayed, and in final settlement of the accounts, more than two years after the election, Mr. Tilden finally reimbursed Mr. Cooper and myself for the excess of our disbursement beyond the subscriptions which we had made. This statement is made in order to correct the impression that Mr. Tilden used a large private fortune in order to secure his election. From facts which are within my knowledge, I

think the money received by him directly was nearly, if not quite, equal to the total amount of his expenditure, including the balance finally paid to Cooper and Hewitt." Nevins, Allen, ed., *Selected Writings of Abram S. Hewitt,* 1937, p. 161.

46. Caldwell, Robert G., *James A. Garfield,* 1931.

47. Smith, Theodore C., *The Life and Letters of James Abram Garfield,* 1925.

48. Josephson, Matthew, *The Politicos, 1865-1896.*

49. Gibbons, Herbert Adams, *John Wanamaker,* 1926.

50. Croly, Herbert, *Marcus Alonzo Hanna,* 1912.

51. Cited in Robinson, William A., *Thomas B. Reed, Parliamentarian,* 1930.

52. Hirsch, Mark D., *William C. Whitney: Modern Warwick,* 1948.

53. *Ibid.,* pp. 239, 330, 49 n. This exceeds the sum Gibbons thought to be largest in 1888.

54. *Ibid.,* p. 508. At least $65,000 was expended in the important and strategic states of Michigan, Indiana, and Kentucky. All of Kentucky's electors but one went to McKinley, the first time Republicans received any electors in this border state.

55. "He constantly helped McKinley by loans, by taking care of notes and by financing of his friend's campaigns." Croly, *op. cit.,* p. 147.

56. A similar action was taken in 1842, to pay the debts of Henry Clay but without his knowledge and consent. It is perhaps significant that proponents and beneficiaries of the protective tariff were large contributors in his case as well.

57. "They had nothing to offer in return for delegates that could not be offered on behalf of another candidate—*viz.* the Federal offices in event of success—but they divined that personal attention means much to Southerners; and they had used most effectively the knowledge." Croly, *op. cit.,* p. 176.

58. Robinson, *op. cit.,* pp. 334-344. Reed referring to the southern delegates declared "They were for me until the buying started." Henry Cabot Lodge agreed.

59. "Reed's bitterness and use of language suggests the views of later southern opponents of civil rights when a seeker of favors from McKinley asked the speaker whether it was expedient for him to see McKinley. Reed replied: 'Well, have you ever bought any Southern delegates for McKinley? I do not mean ordinary delegates, I mean niggers, niggers! If you ever bought any niggers for McKinley then you will probably get what you want; otherwise, I don't think there's much of a chance.' " Robinson, *op. cit.,* pp. 334-5, citing Johnson, Robert Underwood, *Remembered Yesterdays,* 1923, p. 410.

60. Woodward, C. Vann, *Origins of the New South,* 1951, p. 9.

61. Shannon, Jasper, "The Political Process in Kentucky," *Kentucky Law Journal,* XLV (1957), p. 400.

62. Cited in Woodward, *op. cit.,* p. 327.

63. Harris, Joseph P., *Registration of Voters in United States,* 1929, pp. 5-6.

64. "Mark Hanna simply unveiled the springs on which men are manipulated into greatness.
    " 'He had advertised McKinley,' Theodore Roosevelt told my father, 'as if he were a patent medicine!'
    "This was Mr. Hanna's crime. He had openly made use of the full powers of propaganda." Thomas Beer, *Hanna,* 1929, p. 165.

65. Croly, *op. cit.,* p. 219. Emphasis supplied.

66. Bryan, William J., *The First Battle,* 1896, pp. 291-332, *passim.*

67. O'Conner, Harvey, *The Guggenheims,* 1937, pp. 233-246.

68. As quoted in La Follette's *Autobiography,* 1913, pp. 23-24. A leading figure in the Wisconsin Progressive movement, William T. Evjue, still contends that this is the principal issue of our times. See various broadcasts, "Hello, Wis-

consin!" in current issues of Madison, Wisconsin, *Capital Times.*

69. *Ibid.*, p. 197. Also he was impressed by the English Corrupt Practices Act, p. 200.

70. See the account given by Villard, O. G., *Fighting Years*, 1939, pp. 179-181.

71. Morison, Elting, ed., *Letters of Theodore Roosevelt*, 1952.

72. *Ibid.*, p. 68. This celebrated episode is reviewed in detail in Kennan, George, *E. H. Harriman*, 1922, II, pp. 174-227. The situation arose out of the management of funds. The National Committee was to raise money and give part of it to the New York state committee which had insufficient funds. Roosevelt was seeking Harriman's help but Kennan's view is that he deliberately tried to arrange the record so that Harriman was made to appear as taking the initiative for an interview with the President on a campaign fund raising mission.

73. See Lafollette's damaging interpretation of Roosevelt's behavior in his *Autobiography*, pp. 709-728.

74. Pusey, Merlo J., *Charles Evans Hughes*, 1951.

75. Porter, Kirk, *National Party Platforms*, 1936.

76. Pollock, James K., *Party Campaign Funds*, 1926.

77. Pringle, Henry, *Life and Times of William Howard Taft*, 1939, I, pp. 362-3.

78. "The delay (in passing) proved to have been due to the fact that a Democratic House was not elected until 1910. Commencing as a nonpartisan movement, the enactment of a Federal campaign publicity law became, because of the hostile attitude of the Republican leaders in the Senate and House in three Congresses and in its national convention of 1908, notwithstanding their candidates upon approval, an achievement of the Democratic Party." Belmont, *op. cit.*, p. 488.

79. LaFollette, Belle and Fola, *LaFollette*, I, p. 352.

80. Josephson, Matthew, *The President Makers*, 1940. "The angels with money, Medill McCormick, Gifford Pinchot, and Amos Pinchot—the last with some reluctance—now left LaFollette's side for good."—p. 417. See also La-Follette's *Autobiography*, p. 596.

81. Morgenthau, Henry Sr., *All in a Life-Time*, 1922.

82. Link, Arthur, *Wilson: The Road to the White House*, 1947, p. 336.

83. Baker, Ray S., *Woodrow Wilson*. Link puts the figure at slightly over $193,000. The principal sums expended were as follows: (1) Printing, $18,000; (2) Advertising, $12,000; (3) Washington headquarters, $15,000; (4) state leaders, $67,000; (5) office expenses, $22,000. McCombs, Wilson's manager spent prodigally but gave liberally, $11,000 himself. Cleveland Dodge gave in all $51,300 and collected $21,000 from another source. Wilson's old Princeton friends donated a total of about $85,000 or almost half of the entire sum. Link, *op. cit.*, p. 401.

84. Link, *op. cit.*, p. 484. The figures reveal this clearly.

Total gifts	$1,110,052.25
Of 89,854 contributors, 88,229 gave less than	
$100 each	318,909.50
1625 gave more than $100 each	729,042.75
155 gave almost half of the total	508,708.00
40 gave more than $5,000 each	364,950.00

Charles R. Crane, who had financed LaFollette, gave $40,000 while Cleveland Dodge added another $35,000, making his total investment in Wilson almost $90,000. No gifts were accepted from Morgan, Belmont, or Ryan.

85. Harvey, George, *Henry Clay Frick*, 1928.

III THE UNITED STATES EXPERIENCE: SINCE 1916

1. Friedel, Frank, *Franklin D. Roosevelt*, 1952, I, p. 271.

2. Morgenthau, Henry, Sr., *All in a Life-Time*, 1922.

3. Veteran Republicans, some of progressive leanings, were the victims in 1922: McCumber in North Dakota, Cummins

in Iowa, and Harry S. New in Indiana. The Scripps-Howard press took an important part in pushing the issue.

4. The court divided 5-4 with Justice McReynolds for the majority narrowly construing the word "primary" not to be an "election." *U.S. v. Newberry,* 256 U.S. 232 (1924).

5. Hutchinson, William T., *Lowden of Illinois,* 1957. The total was around $415,000 of which $35,000 was donated by friends. The largest amount spent was for printing, $196,000, with $156,000 going for organizational work. A loving and dutiful wife, Mrs. Lowden wrote her husband after his failure to obtain the nomination: "Please darling don't think or speak about that wretched money again. You know that everything I have is just as much yours, and that you couldn't use it in any way that I would not think entirely right." p. 470.

6. Adams, Samuel Hopkins, *Incredible Era,* 1939. "It is ironic that a man [Lowden] so scrupulous about the use of money that he would accept no large contribution for his campaign, preferring to defray the expenses out of his own private purse, should have been the victim of this particular stigma. It killed his chances as surely as the 'fat cat' funds killed General Wood's." p. 138.

7. Hoover, Herbert, *Memoirs,* 1952, II. "Governor Frank Lowden was a man eminently fitted for the Presidency. He should have been nominated in 1920." p. 194.

8. Bowden, Robert, *Boise Penrose,* 1937, pp. 222-242, 259, 260. He had already picked Mellon for the cabinet according to this account.

9. Among other candidates, Hiram Johnson spent $194,393; Hoover, $173,542; Coolidge, $68,375; and Butler, $40,550. Hutchinson, *op. cit.,* p. 454.

10. Wood had borrowed $700,000 of his $1,773,303 from Colonel Proctor. According to one report, a Lowden backer offered to assume the Wood debt to Proctor if Wood would release his delegates to Lowden. Lowden refused. *Ibid.,* p. 467.

11. White, William Allen, *Autobiography,* 1946, p. 584. A widely differing view is presented in Watson, James E., *As I Knew Them,* 1936, pp. 210-11, 219-21.

12. *Memoirs of Will H. Hays,* 1955.

13. White, William Allen, *op. cit.,* p. 584. Certainly in the background the notorious figure of Jake Hamon loomed. First, he spent $100,000 for Wood, then turned his services to Lowden. Hutchinson, *op. cit.,* II, p. 441.

14. Longworth, Alice Roosevelt, *Crowded Hours,* 1933, p. 320.

15. J. Howard Henderson, "Money: It Comes and Goes Unrecorded." *Louisville Courier Journal,* Sept. 28, 1941.

16. Porter, Kirk, *National Party Platforms,* 1936. Emphasis supplied.

17. LaFollette, Belle and Fola, *LaFollette.*

18. *Ibid.,* pp. 1132-3. The meeting took place in Detroit.

19. In view of the Red charges it is of interest that in 1958 Wheeler was offered the Republican nomination for Senator in Montana after he had been previously defeated as too conservative for the Democrats. He had led the opposition to the Roosevelt Supreme Court reform bill of 1937. LaFollette, now deceased three decades, was chosen one of the five most distinguished Senators in United States history.

20. Overacker, Louise, *Money in Elections,* 1932.

21. Wooddy, Carroll, *The Case of Frank L. Smith,* 1930.

22. O'Connor, Harvey, *The Guggenheims,* 1937.

23. Peel, Roy V. and Thomas C. Connelly, *The 1928 Campaign,* 1931.

24. Dabney, Virginius, *Dry Messiah,* 1949, *passim,* but especially pp. 178-189, 252-291.

25. Kane, Harnett T., *Louisiana Hayride,* 1941, *passim.* Especially pp. 73, 96. State employees contributed a flat 10% of their pay for campaign funds.

26. "I will take off my coat and vest and fight to the end any candidate who persists in any demagogic appeal to the masses of the working people of this country to destroy themselves by setting class against class and rich against poor," declared Governor Smith in April 1932. Peel, Roy V. and Thomas C. Connelly, *The 1932 Campaign*, 1935, p. 64.

27. One factor in launching Roosevelt's original career in 1910 was the expectation of the local Democrats that they could hit a "gold mine"; Roosevelt, his friends and mother contributed $2,500. Freidel, Frank, *Franklin D. Roosevelt*, 1952, I, pp. 87-8.

28. Freidel, *op. cit.*, 1956, III, p. 288: "I have given Mr. Howe a cheque for $5,000 out of *principal*, as my income is cut down. He said he *might* not need it now, but I think it would be well for you to tell him that if he has any *extra* money it would be well to keep it until you are nominated. . . . If you are not nominated, I should not *weep*, but it would be money thrown away." Emphasis in original.

29. It was estimated that the 1932 campaign would be the "most inexpensive presidential campaign of two decades." *New York Times*, October 9, 1932.

30. Freidel, *op. cit.*, III, p. 322. The Republicans had more hours of time than the Democrats.

31. Ickes, Harold L., *The Secret Diary of Harold L. Ickes*, II, *The Inside Struggle*, 1954. "Baruch is very generous in his contributions to party funds. As was remarked by the Vice President [Garner] and Jim Farley at cabinet today, he gives money freely but he gives it directly to the beneficiaries. He is not very much interested in members of the House of Representatives but there are quite a number of Democratic Senators on the so-called 'Baruch string'; Swanson related that in the 1932 campaign all he had to do when he needed money was to ask Baruch for it. On one occasion he asked for $25,000 and Baruch sent him $35,000. The Vice President said that Baruch had repeatedly told him to come to him whenever he needed anything but that he had never gone to Baruch. Jim Farley said the same thing."

32. Burns, James M., *Roosevelt: The Lion and the Fox,* 1956.

33. *Hearings* before the *Joint Committee on the Investigation of The Tennessee Valley Authority,* 1939, Part I, pp. 59-94.

34. The circumstances were related to the writer by the late Charles L. West in December 1955, shortly before his death. In 1938 West was one of the six presidential assistants, or "anonyms."

35. A summary is given in Stokes, Thomas L., *Chip Off My Shoulder,* 1940, pp. 534-539. Stokes received a Pulitzer award for his "revelations."

36. Shannon, J. B., "Presidential Politics in the South, 1938," *Journal of Politics,* 1939, I. pp. 166-8. The counties where the WPA was alleged to have corrupted the electorate voted for Chandler in the primary and Republican in November.

37. Harry S. Truman, *Memoirs,* 1956—"I have never been sold on the Hatch Act."

38. The purpose was to prevent Federal office holders from being delegates. *New York Times,* July 30, 1939.

39. Document entitled "Pernicious Political Activities," Senate Document 105, 76th Congress, 1st sess., August 22, 1939.

40. Sec. 13, *Hatch Political Activities Acts,* Public Law No. 753, Senate Doc. No. 264, 76th Congress, 3rd sess., 1940.

41. Truman was opposed by an incumbent governor. The second Hatch Act had the support of the two men who had been opposing candidates in the Kentucky primary of 1938. Governor Chandler had been appointed to the Senate. He was up for reelection in 1940. The chairman of the Kentucky Highway Commission had some ambitions to oust Chandler by use of highway employees and funds collected "voluntarily" from these workers. Chandler candidly advocated the second Hatch Act to keep anyone else from doing to him what he had tried to do to Barkley. He contended that all states would soon have "little" Hatch Acts. In 1955, he ran again for Governor including in his "platform" a provision against "assessment" of state employees.

At the present writing (1958) the practice is still in operation in Kentucky. Two candidates for the Democratic nomination for Governor in 1959 are promising to outlaw the practice.

42. The early prediction that the 1940 amendments to the Hatch Act "had eliminated the potential danger that the destruction of the Federal patronage machine would result only in a transfer of machine politics from the federal to the state units," has not been borne out. "The Historical and Comparative Background of The Hatch Law," in *Public Policy*, 1941, II, p. 362.

43. Minority leader Knowland of California is a case in point. Senator Jenner of Indiana may be another. Chandler in Kentucky deliberately chose the governorship as a way to "come back" in politics rather than the senate. A factor in Governor Williams' seeking an unprecedented sixth term in Michigan follows the same line of reasoning.

44. The writer listened to the Senate debate during the course of the controversy. The overtones of immediate personal, partisan, and factional politics were very evident.

45. The national Democratic leadership of the Senate shrewdly threw considerable financial aid to the Democratic nominee. In 1958, funds to the same candidate were reported to be cut down because of his opposition to measures favored by the Senate Majority Leader.

46. This was part of an economic conflict—probably more economic than political. Galbraith, John Kenneth, *American Capitalism*, 1952, p. 156. "The struggle over the Taft-Hartley Act is an example of the kind of political issue which countervailing power can be expected to develop."

47. "The fact is that he [Louis Johnson] did the job when no one else was willing to take it on." Redding, Jack, *Inside the Democratic Party*, 1958.

48. *Ibid.*, p. 235. "But what the ad agency never knew was that at the time they received our check and delivered theirs to the network, the committee bank account was down to something like five hundred dollars."

49. An astute observer commented, "Two-thirds of these people would be here if Dewey had been elected." *Hearings before Senate Subcommittee on The Establishment of a Commission on Ethics in Government,* 82nd Congress, 1st sess., 1951, p. 45.

50. Davis, Paul T., Malcolm Moos, and Ralph Goldman, *Presidential Nominating Politics in 1952,* 1954, II, *The Northeast.*

51. *Ibid.,* III, *The South.*

52. *Ibid.,* V, *The West.*

53. *Ibid.,* IV, *The Midwest.*

54. The writer watched at first hand the decisive battle between the Eisenhower and Taft forces in the Credentials Committee at Chicago. He is convinced that the showmanship of the Eisenhower delegation from Louisiana was the single most important factor in winning this contest and ultimately the nomination. One can only speculate about the evolution of political parties if Theodore Roosevelt had possessed this medium in the convention of 1912.

55. Candidates for the Democratic nomination for governor in Kentucky in 1955 followed a similar pattern of "pitiless publicity."

56. Testimony of Professor Alexander Heard, in *Hearings* of Subcommittee on Privilege and Elections entitled *1956 Presidential and Senatorial Campaign Contributions and Practices,* 84th Congress, 2nd Sess., 1956, p. 10.

57. *Lincoln Star,* October 8, 1958.

58. Childs, Marquis, "Politics Suffers in Money Battle," *Lincoln Star,* October 13, 1958.

59. *Capital Times,* Madison, Wis., October 10-15, 1958.

60. *Des Moines Register,* October 15, 1958.

IV THE NORWEGIAN EXPERIENCE

1. In 1836, a careful English student concluded: "The Norwegian people enjoy a greater share of political liberty, have the framing and administering of their own laws more entirely in their own hands, than any European nation of the present times." Laing, Samuel, *Journal of a Residence in Norway,* London, 1836.

2. Tønnes Andenaes, ed., *The Constitution of Norway,* 1956, p. 55.

3. Interview September 28, 1954, with Mr. Tønnes Andenaes.

4. *Innstilling Angaende Spørsmalet om a Gjennomføre Offentlighetsprinsippet Nar det Gjelder Finansieringen Av de Politiske Partier og Den Politiske Presse* [*The Question of An Effective Publicity Principle in the Financing of Political Parties and the Party Press*—frequently referred to in this study as *Report on Financing of Parties*], Oslo, 1952, published in response to the Royal resolution of December 23, 1949. "Norwegian legislation contains no rules which regulate the financing of the political parties, or access to give contributions to such parties." p. 43.

5. The writer interviewed politicians from all six Norwegian political parties during the year 1954-55.

6. Interview with Mr. Emil Løvlien, leader of the Communist party in the nation and in Storting, May 7, 1955.

7. Interview with Mr. Carl J. Hambro, then leader of the Conservative party, May 5, 1955.

8. Koht, Halvdan, *Johan Sverdrup,* I, pp. 515-22, III², pp. 548-550. Also, interview with Professor Koht, April 19, 1955.

9. Interview with Professor Koht, April 19, 1955.

10. The expression was Mr. Hambro's.

11. *News of Norway,* V, p. 100; XV, p. 14.

12. In the *Ligningsboka,* Oslo, 1954-55, he was listed with no "fortune" or property and an income of 20,700 kroner as Storting President, the equivalent in United States money of less than $3,500. This was one fifth the income of a fairly well-known Norwegian editor.

13. Lyche, K. C., "Broadcasting," *The Norway Yearbook,* 1954.

14. Lecture by Mr. Karl Lyche to American Fulbright Grantees, University of Oslo, April 21, 1955.

15. *Ibid.* The writer gained the impression that the staff of the Radio Corporation was interested primarily in cultural as distinguished from political adult education.

16. Whereas United States papers gave 60 per cent of their space to advertising, the Norwegian press allocated 40 per cent to advertising. Lecture by Mr. Per Monsen, editor of *Arbeiderbladet,* University of Oslo, October 27, 1954.

17. Vogt, Per, "Press," *Norway Year Book, op. cit.*

18. Interview with Mr. Haakon Lie, Secretary of Labor party, Sept. 15, 1954.

19. Interview with Martin Tranmael, May 13, 1955.

20. Galenson, Walter, *Labor in Norway,* 1949.

21. Interview with Mr. Tor Upsahl, Treasurer and Business Manager of Labor party, May 12, 1955.

22. Bull, Edward, *The Norwegian Trade Union Movement,* 1956 (ICFTU monographs on national trade union movements. No. 4).

23. Interviews with Upsahl, Lie, and others.

24. Interview with Prime Minister Einar Gerhardsen, August 19, 1955.

25. Interview with Finn Moe, Labor Stortingsman, May 5, 1955.

26. This judgment is based upon the opportunity which the writer had to observe the resources of both. Labor officials were more specific than Conservative ones.

27. The General Party Secretary says there are no dues-paying members. Interview with Mr. Leif Helberg, February 23, 1955.

28. Interview with Mr. Ursin, Secretary of the Oslo Branch of Conservative party, February 22, 1955.

29. Interview with Mr. Jens P. Höel, secretary of young people's organization, February 28, 1955.

30. Interview with Fru Fjeldheim, head of Conservative women's organization, March 1, 1955.

31. Interview with Mr. Martin Varvik, Secretary-Treasurer of the Bondepartiet, February 18, 1955.

32. Interview with Mr. Kristian Hansson, executive of Church and Education Department, March 14, 1955.

33. Interview with lawyer Erling Wikborg, leader of the Christian Peoples' party, March 15, 1955.

34. Figures supplied writer by Mr. Kjell Bondevik, Christian party Stortingsman, March 23, 1955. The by-laws of the party require direct members to pay at least five kroner yearly as dues. *Report on Financing of Parties, op. cit.,* p. 15.

35. Wikborg in 1953 was listed with property of over $60,000 and an annual income of approximately $15,000. See *Ligningsboka, op. cit.,* p. 404.

36. Interview with Mr. Arnt Mørland, shipowner and Stortingsman, March 22, 1955. According to tax rolls, Mørland had the largest income of any Stortingsman.

37. Interview with Professor Helge Seip, Liberal Stortingsman, March 24, 1955.

38. Interview with Mr. John Egeland, retired Director of Shipowners Information Organization, April 20, 1955.

39. Figures in *Report on Financing of Parties, op. cit.,* p. 18.

40. The figures of 1947 may have included some donations as well. *Ibid.,* p. 19.

41. Interviews with Mr. Per Bergsvendsen, General Secretary of Venestre, and Mr. Ragnar Sem, Head of Young People's Venestre, August 15, 1955. Badly split into two wings with the shipowners representing the traditional point of view an internal struggle goes on in the party. The largest contributor is a shipowner who gives 10,000 kroner a year. The older group does not like to support financially the young people's organization which in point of view does not differ from the young Labor party organization.

42. Interview with J. P. Höel, already cited. He provided names and cases within his personal knowledge.

43. Interview with a former member of the editorial staff, Mr. Erik Kreyberg, April 29, 1955.

44. *Constitution of Communist Party of Norway*, Sect. 10.

45. Løvlien, the party leader, says it is not true. Other rather well informed people declare each member gives 1,000 kroner a year to the party from his salary.

46. *Report on Financing of Parties, op. cit.*, p. 18.

47. Calculations based on figures given in *Report on Financing of Parties, op. cit.*, pp. 18-21. Precise Communist party figures are not given for 1949.

48. These figures are based on those represented in the *Report on Financing of Parties*, but are not precise. However, their proportions are approximately correct.

49. Interview with lawyer Trygve de Lange and lawyer Sverre Thon, Nov. 22, 1954. The Labor party was the largest one in a coalition government until the election of 1945.

50. The writer was present during the debate as was the author of the *Report*, now a judge. The discussion is reported in *Storting Debates*, March 24, 1955, pp. 699-706.

51. Reprint from the Norwegian weekly *Farmand*, n.d., issued April, 1955.

52. The idea of "good will" advertising was new in Norway. The concept was introduced by a returned Norwegian who had lived many years in the United States. He had learned

about "good will" advertising from a well known American drug firm. Interview with Mr. Leif P. Loennecker, a director of Anth. B. Nilsen and Co., Ltd., March 3, 1955.

53. Business of the firm picked up during the period of advertising. The theory of the firm was that little businessmen feared to criticize the government lest they be penalized. They rejoiced in a larger business saying what they would like to say.

54. Reprint from *Farmand,* January 15, 1957.

55. *Morgan v. Tate & Lyle Ltd.* (1953), 1 W.L.R. 145; (1954) 3 W.L.R. 85. Of special interest is the distinction drawn between what the sugar refinery was permitted to do and the refusal to allow a brewery to make a similar deduction for expenses used in opposing prohibition in New Zealand.

56. Editorial criticizing the view in *Capital Times,* Madison, Wis., July 28, 1958.

57. *Ligningsboka, op. cit.* The price is about $4.00. This publicity feature is reported to have originated in Sweden; at least, Oslo borrowed the practice from Goteborg.

58. The existence of public income-tax returns in Wisconsin was a leading factor in exposing the unusual personal finances of Senator Joseph McCarthy. See *Senate Report on Senators McCarthy and Benton* (photographic reproduction), 1953, pp. 300-306.

59. Since women won the vote no less than 61.8% of the eligible vote has been cast. Since 1936, only once has the percentage of the eligible vote dropped below 75%. In 1953, 76.6% voted. *Statistical Yearbook of Norway,* 1954, p. 300.

60. Duffy, Frank J., *The Political Institutions and Government of Norway* (mimeographed), University of Oslo, 1953, p. 57.

61. Lecture by Mr. Elstad, July 12, 1955, in Oslo on Trade Union Movement. Average wage of worker was 11,000 to 12,000 kroner (approximately $1700) a year.

62. Interview with a member of the Storting who requested that the source of the information be kept confidential. This source said the salary equaled 100,000 kroner in business.

63. *News of Norway,* XV, 98.

64. Discussion of "Concession Laws," *The Norway Year Book,* 1923, pp. 362-366.

65. The writer witnessed this experience in an Institute sponsored by the State Department in the summer of 1955 at Sormarka.

66. Bryce, James, *Modern Democracies,* 1921, II, p. 254.

67. *Ibid.,* I, p. 444.

V   NEW DIRECTIONS

1. Interview with Carl J. Hambro, May 5, 1955.

2. Interview with Professor François Goguel, June 4, 1955. Also, Finer, Herman, *Governments of Greater European Powers,* 1956, p. 350.

3. Personal interview with local Labour party official, Kensington, London, England. May 27, 1955.

4. Interview with Conservative party Treasurer, Mr. Garmonsway, May 21, 1955.

5. *Constituency Finance,* No. 6, Conservative and Unionist Central Office, Organization Series, 1954, p. 6.

6. Wilson, Woodrow, *Leaders of Men,* 1952, p. 20.

7. Something of this nature was suggested in Wallas, Graham, *Human Nature in Politics,* 1908.

8. Roosevelt, Theodore, *Presidential Addresses and State Papers,* 1910, VII, pp. 157-8.

9. Letter to William R. Nelson, July 30, 1912. Morison, Elting, ed., *Letters of Theodore Roosevelt,* 1954, VII, pp. 582-3.

10. Prime Minister Gerhardsen, in an interview in August, 1955, raised this issue and mentioned the multiparty situation in France. See comment of Senator Douglas in *Hearings* before a Senate Subcommittee on The Establishment of a Commission on Ethics in Government, 1951.

11. Personal interview with Mr. Maurice Farquarson of British Broadcasting Corporation, May 26, 1955. The parties themselves made the agreement. Since each candidate must put up 150 pounds which is forfeited if he does not get one-eighth of the vote cast, the financial burden on splinter parties is heavy. To enter fifty candidates would cost about $16,000 alone. The Communist party was kept off the BBC in this fashion in 1955.

12. See Senator Paul Douglas's objection to the American Political Science Association Committee Report, "Towards a More Responsible Two Party System," *Hearings on Ethics,* p. 53.

13. Interview with Mr. Trygve Bratteli, member of Labor government, Oslo, July 12, 1955.

14. Deutscher, Isaac, *Stalin,* 1949, pp. 86-7.

15. Morehead, Alan, *The Russian Revolution,* 1958, pp. 206-10.

16. Galbraith, *American Capitalism,* pp. 115-157.

17. Overacker, Louise, *Presidential Campaign Funds,* 1946, p. 45.

18. Epstein, Leon D., *Politics in Wisconsin,* 1958, p. 28.

19. Compilation based upon *Election Laws,* Research Publication No. 52, Legislative Research Commission, Commonwealth of Kentucky, 1957, pp. 111-2.

20. In Kentucky, a lawsuit has been started to demand an accounting of funds collected from state employees. According to widely published reports employees give monthly contributions from their pay checks similar to income-tax deductions. *Louisville Courier Journal,* January 29-30, 1957. In Indiana the pattern is similar but there it is in the Republican instead of the Democratic party.

21. *Theodore Roosevelt Cyclopedia*, 1941, p. 437.

22. Report entitled *Om Offentlig Redovisning Av Den Politiska Propagandans Finansiering*, Stockholm, 1951. For a discussion of the entire subject based on this report see Fusilier, Raymond, "Les finances des partis politiques," *Review Politique et Parlementaire*, October, 1953, pp. 146-161, and November, 1953, pp. 258-276.

23. Report made to writer by Mr. Marvin McDow, Fulbright exchange teacher to Denmark, 1955-56.

24. For an example see the criticism by Senator Schoeppel of the testimony of Professor Alexander Heard growing out of his statement upon the subject. Reprint from *Congressional Record*, 85th Congress, 1st Sess., pp. 1-29. See the reply of Senator Gore, April 12, 1957, in his defense of his committee.

25. Thorelli, Hans, *The Federal Anti-Trust Policy*, 1954, pp. 246 ff.

26. The writer has developed this theme more extensively in "The Political Process in Kentucky," *supra*.

27. News account of Aerojet General Corporation's "good citizenship campaign." *Louisville Courier-Journal*, October 9, 1958.

28. Part of this suggestion was presented to the Senatorial Committee Studying Ethics in Government under the chairmanship of Senator Paul Douglas in 1951.

29. "The line which divides our area of wealth from our area of poverty is roughly that which divides privately produced and marketed goods and services from publicly rendered services." Galbraith, John K., *Our Affluent Society*, 1958, p. 251.

30. Henry Adams to Perry Belmont, in Belmont, *An American Democrat*, p. 477.